COMMUNION WITH GOD

'The term "Communion", as used by Owen, is used in a wider sense than is consistent with that which is now generally attached to it in religious phraseology. It denotes not merely the interchange of feeling between God in his gracious character and a soul in a state of grace, but the gracious relationship upon which this holy interchange is based. On the part of Christ, for example, all his work and its results are described, from the atonement till it takes effect in the actual justification of the sinner. Fully to comprehend his views on this point, it is needful to bear in mind the meaning under which the word Communion is employed by Owen.'

W. H. Goold in a Prefatory Note in the
Works of John Owen, vol. 2, 1850.

THE TREASURES OF JOHN OWEN

COMMUNION WITH GOD

Abridged and made easy to read by
R. J. K. Law

THE BANNER OF TRUTH TRUST

THE BANNER OF TRUTH TRUST
3 Murrayfield Road, Edinburgh EH 12 6EL
PO Box 621, Carlisle, Pennysylvania 17013, USA

★

© R J K Law 1991
First Published 1991
ISBN 0 85151 607 6

★

Typeset in 10½/12pt Linotron Baskerville
at The Spartan Press Ltd, Lymington, Hants
Printed and bound in Great Britain by
BPCC Hazell Books Ltd
Member of BPCC Ltd
Aylesbury, Bucks, England

Publisher's Preface

The Puritan era in England was distinguished pre-eminently by the rich school of evangelical authors whose writings have had such powerful influence wherever they have been read. Among these men none has been regarded more highly than John Owen, whose works combine biblical insight, theology with spirituality and experimental religion to such a marked degree. As an indication of the value placed upon him by the present publishers it may be noted that the sixteen volumes of his Works (in the Goold edition of 1850–53) have been kept in print on account of their importance ever since they were reprinted in 1965. It is hoped that this availability of the full text of Owen can be continued and what is now being issued for the first time is in no way intended to be a replacement.

Those who have accused Owen of being hard to read have generally been people who lacked the time to read him as he deserves. But considering the extent of his writings even those who wish to read him more fully have often, for the same reason, been unable to become as familiar with him as they would wish. Many cannot read enough to be able to determine which of his books contain his finest work and there can be few alive who have read him all. As a result many of Owen's most important and relevant treatises are little known today. The Rev. R. J. K. Law, the abridger of this text, began his work purely for his own profit and as a memory aid. As he proceeded, he felt more and more like the men of 2 Kings chapter 7 who, discovering the riches of the deserted camp of the Syrians, exclaimed, 'This day is a day of good tidings, and we hold our peace'. The need of others to share in his findings thus led to a change in his original purpose.

After examining the quality and skill of Dr Law's abridgement we have fully shared his enthusiasm for getting the best of Owen into the hands of a far larger number of Christians.

A great deal more of Owen's writing has already been prepared by Dr Law in similar form. It is expected that the reception given to this book will lead to the speedy publication of others. The work which is to be found in this first volume is an admirable starting point for those coming to this Puritan leader for the first time. It will also, however, be a great aid to those who may already have his larger volumes but who need a quicker approach to his teaching on great biblical subjects.

In this abridgement the Bible is quoted throughout in the New King James Version.

Contents

1: *The Saints have Communion with God*

John in his First Epistle tells us in general what this communion with God is. He assures Christians that the fellowship of believers 'is with the Father and with his Son Jesus Christ'. And to impress this doctrine on the minds of his readers, he says, 'truly our fellowship is with the Father and with his Son Jesus Christ' (*I John 1:3*).

Christians in those days were poor and despised. Christian leaders were treated as the filth of the world. So to invite people to become Christians, to join in their fellowship and to enjoy the precious things they enjoyed, seemed to be the height of foolishness.

'What good thing will we get if we join up with these Christians? Are they inviting us to share in their troubles? Do they want us to be persecuted, reviled and scorned and to suffer all kinds of evils?'.

It is with these objections in mind that John writes. Notwithstanding all the disadvantages their fellowship lay under from a worldly point of view, yet in truth it was, and they would soon find it to be, very honourable, glorious and desirable. For 'truly,' says John, 'our fellowship is with the Father and with his Son Jesus Christ'.

From this declaration of John, we learn that the saints of God have communion or fellowship with God. And this communion is a holy and spiritual communion, as we shall see.

Because of sin, no man in his natural state has fellowship with God. God is light, and we are darkness. What communion has light with darkness? God is life; we are dead. God is love; we are enmity. So what agreement can there be between

God and man? Men, in such a condition, do not have Christ, and so they are without hope and without God in the world (*Eph. 2:12*). They are 'alienated from the life of God through the ignorance that is in them' (*Eph. 4:18*). Two cannot walk together unless they agree with each other (*Amos 3:3*). Whilst there is this great distance between God and man, there can be no walking together in fellowship or communion. Our first relationship with God was so lost by sin that there was no possibility in ourselves of any return to God.

Now the only way back into fellowship with God is through faith in Jesus Christ. And while Old Testament believers had communion with God through this means, they did not have a boldness and confidence in that communion. The way to the holiest was not yet open (*Heb. 9:8*). Under the New Testament, this way into the holiest has been opened and believers have boldness and confidence to come into God's presence (*Eph. 3:12; Heb. 10:20; Eph. 2:13, 14, 18*). Christ, then, is the foundation of all our communion with God and by the Spirit believers now receive boldness of faith. Consider how greatly God has honoured us!

Human wisdom sees such an infinite disparity between God and man that it concludes there can be no communion between them. The knowledge that God and man can live in fellowship together is hidden in Christ. It is too wonderful for sinful, corrupted human nature to discover. Human wisdom leads only to terrors and fears when it thinks of coming into God's presence. But we have, in Christ, the way into God's presence without fear.

Now communion is the mutual sharing of those good things which delight all those in that fellowship. This was so with David and Jonathan. Their souls were bound together in love (*I Sam. 20:17*). Their love for one another was shown in various ways. But their love was nothing in comparison to the love that is between God and his people. This fellowship

[2]

of love is far more wonderful. Those who enjoy this communion are gloriously united to God through Christ and share in all the glorious and excellent fruits of such communion.

Our communion with God lies in his giving himself to us and our giving ourselves and all that he requires to him. This communion with God flows from that union which is in Christ Jesus.

This communion will be perfect and complete when we enter into the full enjoyment of Christ's glory. Then we shall totally give ourselves up to him, resting in him as the utmost fulfilment of all our desires.

This communion is now only partial because we presently only enjoy the first-fruits and dawnings of that future perfection. It is with regard to this initial communion that I intend to speak and to show that mutual giving and receiving between God and the saints as they walk together in holy and spiritual peace. This covenant of peace is brought about by the blood of Jesus. But first I pray that the God and Father of our Lord Jesus Christ who has, by the riches of his grace, brought us from a state of enmity into this glorious fellowship with himself, may give you such a taste of his sweetness and excellence in this communion as to be stirred up to a greater longing for that eternal enjoyment of him in eternal glory.

2: *Communion with each Person of the Godhead Individually*

The Apostle John tells us, 'There are three that bear witness in heaven, the Father, the Word and the Holy Spirit' (*I John 5:7*). And to what do they bear witness? They bear witness to the Sonship of Christ and the salvation of believers in his blood. John is writing of that salvation by blood and water, symbolising justification and sanctification. Now how do these three persons bear witness to this salvation? They bear witness as three individual, separate witnesses. When God witnesses to our salvation, surely it is incumbent upon us to receive his testimony. The Father bears witness, the Son bears witness and the Holy Spirit bears witness for they are three separate, individual witnesses. So we are to receive each of their testimonies, and as we do so, we have communion with each person of the Godhead severally. In this giving and receiving of this testimony lies a great part of our fellowship with God.

The Apostle Paul, speaking of the distribution of gifts and graces to the saints, shows that they are from each of the persons of the Godhead. In I Corinthians 12:4, he says, 'Now there are diversities of gifts, but the same Spirit' – that one and the selfsame Spirit who is the Holy Spirit. Verse 11: 'There are differences of ministries, but the same Lord' – the same Lord Jesus. Verse 5: 'And there are diversities of activities, but it is the same God who works all in all'. This is the Father (*Eph. 4:6*).

And not only in the flowing forth of grace from God and the works of the Spirit on us, but also in the way we come to God the same distinction is made. Paul says, 'For through him we both have access by one Spirit to the Father' (*Eph. 2:18*). Our access to God, in order that we might have communion with him, is 'through Christ', 'by the Spirit', 'to the Father'. Each person of the Godhead is here considered as having a distinct and separate part to play in accomplishing the purpose of God's will revealed in the gospel.

Sometimes the Father and the Son are especially mentioned (*I John 1:3*). The word 'and' in that verse both distinguishes and unites. (Cf. John 14:23.) The Father and the Son, by making their home with the soul, have communion with that soul.

Sometimes only the Son is mentioned (*I Cor. 1:9; Rev. 3:20*).

Sometimes in this matter of communion only the Spirit is mentioned (*II Cor. 13:14*).

This spiritual and holy communion of the saints with each person of the Godhead is very clear in Scripture.

Faith, love, trust, joy and all other spiritual graces are the means by which the soul has communion with God. These graces are drawn from the soul by prayers and praises which God has appointed for his worship. The Bible clearly shows that by these graces the saints have communion with each person of the Godhead.

Communion with the Father. Faith, love, trust, joy and obedience are the saints' responses to the Father's loving acts shown to them. The Father testifies to and bears witness of his Son (*I John 5:9*). In his bearing witness, the Father is to be believed and trusted. When the Father testifies to his Son, his testimony is to be received by faith. 'He that believes on the Son of God has the witness in himself' (*I John 5:10*). To believe on the Son of God is to receive the Lord Christ as the Son, the Son given to us to fulfil in us the purposes of the Father's love. And we receive the Lord Christ as the Son given to us on the truthfulness of the Father's witness. So

[5]

when we receive this testimony, we put our faith specially in the Father. So John warns, 'He that believes not God,' that is, the Father who bears witness to the Son, 'has made him a liar'. 'You believe in God,' says our Saviour (*John 14:1*). Here he is referring to the Father, for he adds, 'Believe also in me'. God is the first truth upon whose authority all truth is based, and on whose authority all divine faith ultimately rests. In this sense, God is not to be thought of as any one person, but as the whole deity, Father, Son and Holy Spirit. So the triune God is the chief object of faith. But in John 14:1 it is the testimony and authority of the Father which concerns us and on which faith is specially fixed. If our faith was not there directed to the Father, the Son could not add, 'Believe also in me'.

The same is also said of love. John writes, 'If any man love the world, the love of the Father is not in him' (*I John 2:15*). The love of the Father is our love for the Father and not his love for us. In this instance, the Father is put as the object of our love, and is not the cause of our love. And this love given to God as Father is that which he calls his 'honour' (*Mal. 1:6*).

Still further, these graces are seen in our prayers and praises and in our worship which is specially given to the Father. Peter says, 'You call on the Father' (*I Pet. 1:17*). Paul says, 'For this cause I bow my knees to the Father of our Lord Jesus Christ of whom the whole family in heaven and earth is named' (*Eph. 3:14, 15*). 'Bowing the knee' sums up the whole worship of God (*Isa. 45:23*). Verses 24–25 go on to show that this worship lies in acknowledging God as our righteousness and strength. This worship, described as bowing the knee, is directed by Paul distinctly to the Father of our Lord Jesus Christ, the fountain and source of all good things which come to us in Christ. In other places, Paul both joins together and at the same time distinguishes between the

[6]

Father and the Son in his prayers and also in his thanksgivings (*I Thess. 3:11; Eph. 1:3, 4*).

Communion with the Son. Jesus said, 'You believe in God, believe also in me' (*John 14:1*). 'Believe' also includes putting faith in Christ personally as the Son, that same divine supernatural faith with which we believe in God, that is, the Father. There must be a believing about Christ, namely, that he is the Son of God, the Saviour of the world. Jesus threatened the Pharisees for not believing this fact (*John 8:24*). In this sense, faith is not directly fixed on the Son because this 'believing' is only recognising the truth that he is Christ, the Son of God, on the testimony of the Father concerning Jesus. But there is also a believing 'in' Jesus, called 'believing in the name of the Son of God' (*I John 5:13; John 9:36*). This 'believing' is a putting our trust and confidence in the Lord Jesus Christ, the Son of God, as the Son of God (*John 3:16*). The Son, whom the Father gave, is to be trusted as the one that gives us everlasting life and who will keep us from perishing. 'He who believes in him is not condemned' (*John 3:18*). 'He who believes in the Son has everlasting life' (*John 3:36*). 'This is the work of God that you believe in him whom he sent' (*John 6:29, 40; I John 5:10*). The sum of all this is, 'that all men should honour the Son, even as they honour the Father. He that does not honour the Son, does not honour the Father who sent him.'

Love for the Lord Jesus Christ is love for him as God and it therefore includes love for him in religious worship. Only where there is such love does the apostolic benediction belong: 'Grace be with all those that love our Lord Jesus Christ in sincerity' (*Eph. 6:24*).

Faith, hope and love, expressed in obedience and in worship, are especially due to the Son of God from the saints. We see this in the book of Revelation (*Rev. 1:5, 6; 5:8, 13, 14*). The Father and the Son, that is, he that sits on the throne

[7]

and the Lamb, are together yet distinctly given divine worship and honour for ever and ever. And therefore Stephen, in his solemn dying prayer, fixed his faith and hope especially on the Son (*Acts 7:59, 60*). Stephen knew that the Son of man had power to forgive sins also. And this worship of the Lord Jesus, the apostle Paul declares, is the distinguishing characteristic of the saints (*I Cor. 1:2*). 'Calling on the name of God' generally means the whole worship of God. So to call on the name of Jesus Christ is to give all worship to Christ, which is due to him because he is God, the Son.

Communion with the Holy Spirit. All worship is due also to the Holy Spirit, as he is God and as he is the Spirit of grace. The great sin of unbelief is still described as opposition to, and a resisting of, the Holy Spirit. So the Spirit is entitled to all instituted worship, as we see from the appointment of the administration of baptism in his name (*Matt. 28:19*).

So we see that there is no exercise of grace towards God, no act of divine worship given to him, no duty or obedience done for him, but they are distinctly directed to the Father, Son and Spirit. Now in these and in ways similar to these, we have communion or fellowship with God. Therefore we have communion also with each person of the Godhead individually.

We may see this more clearly if we consider how each person of the Godhead communicates to the saints these good things by which they have communion with God. This is seen in two ways:

(1) It is seen when the same things, such as grace and peace, are at the same time attributed jointly and yet distinctly to all the persons of the Godhead and respectively to each of them. The seven Spirits before the throne are the Holy Spirit of God, considered as the source of every perfect gift and dispensation (*Rev. 1:4, 5*). All the persons of the

Godhead are here joined together, and yet all are mentioned separately in their communication of grace and peace to the saints.

(2) It is seen when the same thing is attributed separately to each person of the Godhead. There is, indeed, no gracious influence from above, no entry of light, life, love or grace into our hearts but it comes from the divine order of men's affairs. I shall give only one instance, which is very comprehensive, and may be thought to include all other instances, and this is teaching. The teaching of God is the real communication of everything that comes from God himself to the saints and of which they are made partakers. That promise, 'They shall all be taught of God', includes in itself the whole mystery of grace to us so far as we are made real possessors of it. Now this is attributed to each of the persons of the Godhead.

Teaching is attributed to the Father. The fulfilment of that promise, 'they shall all be taught of God,' is specially meant of the Father. Jesus said, 'It is written in the prophets, "And they shall all be taught of God". Therefore everyone who has heard and learned from the Father comes to me' (*John 6:45*). This teaching, by which we are brought from death to life through faith in Christ, in order that we may be partakers of his life and his love, is of and from the Father. We listen to the Father. We learn from the Father. By the Father, we are brought into union and communion with the Lord Jesus. The Father draws us to Christ. He begets us anew of his own will, by his own Spirit. In this work, the Father uses the ministers of the gospel (*Acts 26:17, 18*).

Teaching is attributed to the Son. The Father proclaims from heaven that his Son is to be the great teacher. 'This is my beloved Son; hear him.' The whole of Christ's prophetic, and no small part of his kingly office lies in 'teaching'. By this teaching, Christ is said to draw men to himself, as the Father is said to do in his teaching (*John 12:32*). Christ does this work with such power that 'the dead hear his voice and live'. The teaching of the Son is a life-giving, a Spirit-breathing teaching. It is an effective influence of light by which Christ shines into darkness. Christ gives life, raising the dead. Christ opens blind eyes and changes hard hearts. Christ pours out the Spirit with all the results of that outpouring. So Christ claims it as his privilege to be the only Master (*Matt. 23:10*).

Teaching is attributed to the Spirit. The Holy Spirit also has a teaching office (*John 14:26; I John 2:27*). That teaching unction which is not only true, but truth itself, is the Holy Spirit of God. So the Holy Spirit also teaches. The Holy Spirit is given to us 'that we might know the things that are freely given to us by God' (*I Cor. 2:12*).

This then further drives home the truth that we are demonstrating. There is a communication of grace to us from each of the persons of the Godhead. This being so, the saints must then have communion with each person of the Godhead distinctly.

But there is this difference with each of the persons of the Godhead. The Father communicates with us on the basis of his being the origin of all authority. The Son communicates with us out of a purchased treasury. The Holy Spirit communicates with us by direct personal working in us.

The Father communicates all grace to us by his own authoritative will (*John 5:21; James 1:18*). Life-giving power is vested in the Father. Therefore in sending the Spirit to give us life, Christ is said to do it from the Father (*John 14:26; 15:26*). But Christ also sends the Spirit himself (*John 16:7*).

The Son communicates to us out of a purchased treasury. 'Of his fulness have all we received' (*John 1:16*). And from where has Christ got this fulness? 'It pleased the Father that in him all fulness should dwell' (*Col. 1:19*). And Paul tells us why that fulness was committed to Christ (*Phil. 2:8–11*).

Christ also has authority to communicate his fulness to us (*John 5:25–27; Matt. 28:18*).

The Spirit communicates to us by directly working in us by his power. Romans 8:11: 'But if the Spirit of him who raised Jesus from the dead dwells in you, he who raised Christ from the dead will also give life to your mortal bodies through his Spirit who dwells in you.'

In this text, we see all the persons of the Godhead agreeing to raise us from death to life.

Here we see the Father's authoritative raising of Jesus from the dead and his giving life to our mortal bodies.

Here we see the Son's mediatory work. It is through his death that our bodies shall be raised from death.

Here we see the Spirit's direct work, for by his dwelling in us, the Father will give life to our mortal bodies.

So we have proved and demonstrated that saints have communion with each person of the Godhead.

3: *Communion with God the Father*

The chief way by which the saints have communion with the Father is love – free, undeserved, eternal love. This love the Father pours on the saints. Saints are to see God as full of love to them. They are to receive him as the One who loves them, and are to be full of praise and thanksgiving to God for his love. They are to show gratitude for his love by living a life which pleases him.

This is the great truth of the gospel. Commonly, the Father, the first person in the Trinity, is seen as only full of wrath and anger against sin. Sinful men can have no other thoughts of God (*Rom. 1:18; Isa. 33:13, 14; Hab. 1:13; Psa. 5:4–6; Eph. 2:3*). But in the gospel, God is now revealed especially as love, as full of love to us. To bring home to us this great truth is the special work of the gospel (*Titus 3:4*).

God is love. In I John 4:8 'God' refers to the Father. This is clear from the following verse, where God is seen as distinct from his only-begotten Son whom he sends into the world. 'Now,' says John, 'the Father is love. He is not only infinitely gracious, tender, compassionate and loving in his nature, but also he is One who gives himself supremely and especially to us freely in love.' So John declares this in the following verses. 'This is love, this is that which I would have you especially to note about the Father. The Father shows his love to you in sending his only-begotten Son into the world that we might live through him' (*v. 9*). 'The Father loved us and sent his Son to be the propitiation for our sins' (*v. 10*). And what is especially to be noted is that God's love for us was before all that Christ has purchased for us (*Eph. 1:4–6*).

Love is distinctly ascribed to God the Father. In II Corinthians 13:14, Paul ascribes grace to our Lord Jesus Christ, fellowship to the Holy Spirit, but love to God the Father. The fellowship of the Spirit is mentioned with the grace of Christ and the love of God, because it is by the Spirit alone that we have fellowship with Christ in grace, and with the Father in love.

The Father himself loves us. In John 16:26, 27, Jesus said, 'I do not say that I shall pray the Father for you; for the Father himself loves you, because you have loved me, and have believed that I came forth from God.'

But doesn't Jesus contradict himself? Has he not plainly said, 'I will pray the Father for you' (*John 14:16*)?

Jesus had spoken many gracious words to his disciples. He had given them many comforting and faithful promises. He had revealed heavenly truths to them. So they were fully convinced of his great love for them and that he would continue to care for them. They knew that he would not forget them when he had gone from them back into heaven. But now all their thoughts were on the Father. How would he accept them? How would he treat them?

Jesus, in effect, says, 'Don't worry about that. I do not have to pray that the Father may love you, for this is his special attitude towards you. He himself loves you. It is true indeed that I will pray the Father to send you the Spirit, the Comforter. But as for that free, eternal love, there is no need for me to pray for that, because above all things the Father loves you. Be fully assured in your hearts that the Father loves you. Have fellowship with the Father in his love. Have no fears or doubts about his love for you. The greatest sorrow and burden you can lay on the Father, the greatest unkindness you can do to him is not to believe that he loves you.'

The Holy Spirit sheds abroad in our hearts the love of God. In Romans 5:5, Paul says, 'The love of God has been poured out in our hearts by the Holy Spirit who was given to us'. God,

[13]

whose love this is, is clearly distinguished from the Holy Spirit who pours out his love. In Romans 5:8, God is clearly distinguished from the Son, for it is from the love of God that the Son is sent. Therefore Paul is speaking of the Father. And what is it that Paul especially ascribes to the Father? It is love. Paul declares God's love to us in this wonderful way in order that we may wake up to it and wholeheartedly believe it and receive it. To impress this truth on us, Paul calls the Father 'the God of love' (*II Cor. 13:11*). John tells us that God is love and that whoever wishes to know God or to dwell in fellowship with God, must dwell in him as he is love (*I John 4:8, 16*).

In God there are two sorts of love. There is his love of good pleasure and his determination to do good, and also a love of friendship and acceptance.

It was his love of good pleasure and his determination to do good that was the reason why he sent his only-begotten Son (*John 3:16; Rom. 9:11, 12; Eph. 1:4, 5; II Thess. 2:13, 14; I John 4:8, 9*).

Then there is his love of friendship and acceptance. 'If anyone loves me,' says Christ, 'he will keep my word; and my Father will love him, and we will come to him and make our home with him' (*John 14:23*). The love of friendship and acceptance is especially ascribed to the Father. Christ says, 'We will come,' that is the Father and the Son, 'to such a one and dwell with him,' that is, by the Spirit. Yet in all this, Christ would have us take note that in the matter of love, the Father has a special right or privilege. 'My Father will love him.'

This love is especially to be recognised as in God. So this love of the Father is to be seen as the fountain or source of all other acts of God's grace to us.

Christians are often very worried as to whether God loves them or not. They are fully persuaded of Christ's love and good-will to them, but the difficulty they have is whether the Father accepts them and loves them. Philip said, 'Lord, show us the Father, and it is sufficient for us' (*John 14:8*). Such thoughts ought to be far from us. The Father's love ought to be looked on as the source from which all other loves flow. Paul said to Titus, 'But when the kindness and the love of God our Saviour towards man appeared . . .' (*Titus 3:4*). He is here speaking of the Father's love, for he goes on to say that that love revealed itself in his mercy in saving us through the washing of regeneration and renewing of the Holy Spirit whom he poured out on us abundantly through Jesus Christ our Saviour (*vv. 5, 6*). It is this love of the Father to which Paul points us that brought us into our present state of being saints, for Paul reminds us that 'we ourselves were also once foolish, disobedient, deceived, serving various lusts and pleasures, living in malice and envy, hateful and hating one another' (*v. 3*). But what brought the great change in us? It was 'the kindness and love of God our Saviour' (*v. 4*). And how did that kindness and love of God show itself? Why, it showed itself in his merciful salvation and the washing of regeneration and renewing of the Holy Spirit, whom he poured out on us abundantly through Jesus Christ our Saviour.

In order to assure us of his love to us, the Father compares himself to a father, a mother, a shepherd, a hen protecting her chicks and the like (*Psa. 103:13; Isa. 63:16; Matt. 6:6; Isa. 66:13; Psa. 23:1; Isa. 40:11; Matt. 23:37*). No further proof is needed. So we can clearly say that there is in the person of the Father a special love to the saints by which he has communion with them.

If we are to have communion with the Father in love, two things are required of us. We must receive the love of the Father, and we must show gratitude and love to the Father.

Believers must receive the love of the Father. Communion or fellowship lies in giving and receiving. Until the love of the Father is received, we have no communion with the Father in love. How then is this love of the Father to be received in order that we may have fellowship with him? There is only one way and that is by faith. To receive the love of the Father is to believe that he does love us. God has so fully, so clearly revealed his love, that it may be received by faith. 'You believe in God,' said Jesus (*John 14:1*). Jesus is here referring to the Father. And what is that which is to be believed in the Father? His love is to be believed, for God is love (*I John 4:8*).

It is true that we do not come directly to the Father by faith. We can only come to him by the Son. Jesus said, 'I am the way, the truth, and the life. No one comes to the Father except through me' (*John 14:6*). Christ is the merciful high priest over the house of God, by whom we have access to the throne of grace. By Christ we have access and acceptance with the Father. By Christ we believe in God (*I Pet. 1:21*). Through Christ, then, we have access to the Father, we behold the Father's glory also and enjoy fellowship with the Father in his own special love. All this we receive by faith. As we come to the Father's love through Christ, so the Father's love comes to us through Christ. The light of the sun comes to us by its beams. By its beams we see the sun, and by its beams the sun touches us. Jesus Christ is the beam of his Father's love and through him the Father's love reaches down and touches us. By Jesus Christ also we see and experience and are led up to the Father's love. If we, as believers, would meditate on this truth more and live in the light of it, there would be great spiritual growth in our walk with God.

This growth in our walk with God is what we are to aim at. Many dark and disturbing thoughts arise to hinder our walk with God. Few can rise to the height of the Father's love by faith, so as to rest their souls in his love. They live far below it in the troublesome region of hopes and fears, storms and clouds. Abiding in the Father's love, all is peace and quiet. But how to rise up to the height of the Father's love they do not know. It is God's will that he should always be seen as gentle, kind, tender, loving and unchangeable. It is his will that we see him as the Father, and the great fountain and reservoir of all grace and love. This is what Christ came to reveal. Christ came to reveal God as a Father (*John 1:18*). It is the name of God as Father which Christ declares to those who are given him out of the world (*John 17:6*). And this is what Christ leads us to, because he is the only way of going to God as a Father (*John 14:5, 6*). He leads us to God as love. By this, Christ gives us the rest which he promised us. We believe in God through Christ (*I Pet. 1:21*). Faith seeks out a place for the soul to rest. This rest is presented to the soul by Christ, the Mediator. By Christ the soul has access into the Father's love (*Eph. 2:18*). Believers find that God is love, and that he loved them from eternity. Believers learn that it was God's will and purpose to love them from everlasting to everlasting in Christ, and that all reason for God to be angry with us and treat us as his enemies has been taken away. The believer, being brought by Christ into the bosom of the Father, rests in the full assurance of God's love and of never being separated from that love. This is the first act of communion which the believer has with the Father.

The response from us that God looks for, in return for his love, is love. God says to us, 'My son, give me your heart' (*Prov. 23:26*). And God commands us to love him with all our heart, soul, strength and mind (*Luke 10:27*). This is the response God wants from us in return for his love to us. When the believer sees God as love, sees him to be infinitely lovely and loving, and finds rest and peace for his soul in that love, then the believer has communion with the Father in love. This is love, that God loves us first, and then we love him in response to his love. Love is a feeling or emotion of union and delight and desire to be near to the object loved. So long as the Father is seen as harsh, judging and condemning, the soul is filled with fear and dread every time it comes to him. So in Scripture we read of sinners fleeing and hiding from him. But when God, who is the Father, is seen as a father, filled with love, the soul is filled with love to God in return. This is, in faith, the ground of all acceptable obedience (*Deut. 5:10; 10:12; 11:1, 13; 13:3; Exod. 20:6*).

Paul tells us that God in his love chose us in Christ before the foundation of the world in order that we should be holy and without blame before him (*Eph. 1:4*). It all begins in the love of God and ends in our love to him. That is what the eternal love of God aims to produce in us.

In order that this communion with the Father in love may be made more clear, two things must be considered. We must consider how this love of God to us and our love to God are similar and how they differ.

HOW GOD'S LOVE TO US AND OUR LOVE TO GOD ARE SIMILAR

God's love to us and our love to God are similar in two ways.

Firstly, they are both a love of rest, contentment and delight.

The love of God is a love of rest, contentment and delight. 'He will rest in his love' (*Zeph. 3:17*). Literally, the Hebrew is, 'He shall be silent because of his love'. To rest with contentment is expressed by being silent, that is, without grumbling and complaining. Because God's love is so full, so perfect and so absolute, it will not allow him to complain of anything in those whom he loves. So he is silent. When God is said to 'rest in his love,' it means he is satisfied with the object of his love and will not seek for a more satisfying object to love. His love will make its home in the soul on which it is fixed for ever. This verse also shows God as delighting in the object of his love. He rejoices as one that is fully satisfied in the object he has chosen to love. There are two Hebrew words expressing the delight and joy he has in his love. One denotes the inward emotion or feeling of the mind and joy of heart. It sets out the intensity or strength of his love. It is a love of gladness and joy. This is the highest expression of delight in love. The inner feeling of delight and joy is expressed outwardly, and God shows his delight with a joyful sound or with singing. When God would show the opposite of this love, he says, 'He was not pleased' (*I Cor. 10:5*). He did not delight in them and nor could his love find rest and contentment in them. We are also told that the soul of the Lord has no pleasure in those who turn back to their old ways (*Heb. 10:38; Jer. 22:28; Hos. 8:8; Mal. 1:10*). God takes pleasure in those that stick close by him. There is rest and delight in God's love. God wills to do good to us, and he rests content in that will. Some say 'to love' is from two Greek words which mean rest and contentment in the object loved. So when God calls his Son 'beloved', he adds, 'in whom I am well pleased', that is, 'in whom I can rest in perfect contentment'.

The saints' love to God in response to God's love for them is also a love of rest, contentment and delight. David says, 'Return to your rest, O my soul, for the Lord has dealt bountifully with you' (*Psa. 116:7*). David makes God his resting place. He is so content with God as his resting place that he has no desire to look for another. 'Whom have I in heaven but you?' asks David. 'And there is none upon earth that I desire besides you' (*Psa. 73:25*). The soul stops all its wanderings and searchings to rest in God alone. The soul chooses the Father for its present and eternal rest. David does this with delight. 'Because your loving-kindness is better than life,' says David, 'my lips shall praise you' (*Psa. 63:3*). David sees God as better than life itself with all its joys. Seeing himself in the jaws of death, rolling into the grave through innumerable troubles, yet he found more sweetness in God than in a long life under its best and most noble conditions, with all the enjoyments that make life pleasant and comfortable. An example of this is given in Hosea: 'Assyria will not save us, we will not ride on horses, nor will we say any more to the work of our hands, "You are our gods", for in you the fatherless finds mercy' (*Hos. 14:3*). They reject the best appearances of rest and contentment, to find it all in God, on whom they cast themselves as if they were helpless orphans.

The mutual love of God and the saints are similar also in that their communion of love is in Christ and through Christ. The Father communicates all his love to us through Christ and we pour out our love to the Father only through Christ. Christ is the treasury in which the Father places all the riches of his grace taken from the bottomless mine of his eternal love. Christ is the priest into whose hand we put all the offerings that we wish to give to the Father. So God's first and chief love is his Son, not only as his eternal Son who was the delight of his soul before the foundation of the world, but also as the Son is our Mediator and the means by which the Father's love is conveyed to us (*Matt. 3:17; John 3:35; 5:20; 10:17; 15:9; 17:24*). In Scripture we are said to have access to God and to believe in God only through Christ.

The Father loves us and 'chose us before the foundation of the world'. And that love of the Father led him to 'bless us with every spiritual blessing in the heavenly places in Christ' (*Eph. 1:3, 4*). From his love, the Father sheds or pours out the Holy Spirit richly upon us through Jesus Christ our Saviour (*Titus 3:6*). In the pouring out of his love, there is not one drop falls on us except through Christ. The holy anointing oil was all poured on the head of Aaron, and from there went down to the skirts of his clothing (*Psa. 133*). So love is first poured out on Christ and from him it flows down to us. The Father's purpose is that Christ should have 'in all things the pre-eminence' (*Col. 1:18*). It is the Father's pleasure that 'in Christ all fulness should dwell', and that 'of his fulness we might receive, and grace for grace' (*Col. 1:19; John 1:16*). Though the love of the Father's purpose and good pleasure are founded on his mere grace and will, yet God purposed that his love would only be poured out on us in and through Christ. All the fruits of God's love are first given to Christ. Christ then gives them to us. Love in the Father is like honey in the flowers. It must be in the comb before we can make use of it. So Christ must extract and prepare the honey of God's love for us.

Christ is the well of salvation into which the water of God's love is poured. We then draw by faith from Christ, the well of salvation, the water of God's love.

The saints' love to God is also in Christ and by Christ. What lame and blind sacrifices would we otherwise present to God! Christ bears the iniquity of our offerings and he adds incense to our prayers. Our love is fixed on the Father. But it is conveyed to the Father through the Son. Christ is the only way for our graces as well as our persons to go to God. Through him, all our desires and delights, our satisfactions and our obedience pass to the Father.

HOW THE LOVE OF THE FATHER TO THE SAINTS AND THE LOVE OF THE SAINTS TO THE FATHER DIFFER

The love of God is a sovereign love, freely given. Our love to God is a love which we are duty-bound to give.

The love of the Father is sovereign and freely given. It is a love which fills God with desires to do good and great things to and for us. The Father's love is behind everything he does for us. He loves us and sends his Son to die for us. He loves us and blesses us with every spiritual blessing. Loving is choosing (*Rom. 9:11, 12*). But his love is also disciplinary.

God's love is like the heavens when, full of rain, they pour down showers to make the earth fruitful. The Father's love is like a bubbling spring or a sparkling fountain, always pouring out water. The Father's love powerfully beautifies the object on which his love is poured, infusing into and creating goodness in the persons loved. He that loves desires only to do good to the object of his love. God's power and will are one. They work together. What God wills he powerfully works.

Our love to God is a love which we are bound to give. It is the love of a child. God's love comes down to us freely and richly. Our love ascends to him in duty and gratitude. God adds to us by his love. We add nothing to him by our love. Though our love is fixed directly on the Father, yet no actual fruit of our love reaches him direct from us, but only through Christ. Though the Father requires our love, he is not benefited by it (*Job 35:5–8; Rom. 11:35; Job 22:2, 3*).

Our love to God is made up of rest, delight, reverence and obedience. By these we have fellowship with the Father in his love. So God calls that love which is due to him as a Father 'his honour' (*Mal. 1:6*). 'If then I am the Father, where is my honour?'. Our love, then, is an act of duty to God which he deserves from us.

The father's love to us differs from our love to him in this also: the Father's love to us precedes our love to the Father. Our love to the Father is the result of the Father's love to us.

The father loves the child when the child does not know the father, much less loves him. It is the same with us (*I John 4:10*). We are, by nature, 'haters of God' (*Rom. 1:30*). God in his own nature is a lover of men. So God's love must precede ours.

The Father's love precedes all other reasons for loving. The Father's love not only precedes our love but also anything that is lovely in us. 'But God demonstrates his own love towards us, in that while we were still sinners, Christ died for us' (*Rom. 5:8*). Not only the Father's love, but all the wonderful works arising from that love are brought to us while we are still sinners. Sin makes the sinner unlovely and undesirable. There is nothing in the sinner that could arouse love in God. Yet it is as sinners that God loves us. Not only when we had done no good, but when we were polluted in our own blood (*Ezek. 16:6*). God loved us, and that, not because we were better than others, but because he himself is infinitely good. His kindness appeared when we were foolish and disobedient. So God is said to 'love the world', that is, those who have nothing but what is in and of the world, which lies in the hands of the evil one.

Our love responds to God's love. No sinner ever turned his heart to God if the heart of God were not first set on the sinner.

God must be revealed to us as lovely and desirable, as a fit and suitable object of rest to the soul, before we can ever love God. The saints, in this sense, do not love God for nothing. They love him for his loveliness and because he is so desirable. The Psalmist says, 'I love the Lord, because he has heard my voice and my supplications' (*Psa. 116:1*). So also we may say, 'We love the Lord, because . . . !'. Or as David said, 'What have I done now? Is there not a cause?' (*I Sam. 17:29*). So if anyone asks about our love to God, we may say, 'What have we done now? Is there not a cause?'

The love of the Father to the saints and the love of the saints to the Father differ in this also. The love of God is like himself. His love is the same for all he has chosen to love. His love is constant and not capable of being increased or diminished. Our love is like ourselves, never the same, but increasing or

[23]

decreasing, growing or declining. God's love is like the sun, always the same in its light, though a cloud may sometimes hide it. Our love is like the moon. Sometimes it is full. Sometimes it is only a thin crescent.

The love of the Father is the same for all whom he has chosen to love. Whom God loves he loves to the end, and he loves them all alike. On whom he sets his love, it is set for ever. God's love does not grow to eternity or lessen in time. God's love is an eternal love that had no beginning and that shall have no end. It is a love that cannot be increased by anything we do and that cannot be lessened by anything in us.

But the love of God may be seen to be changeable in two ways:

(1) God's love is changeable in its communications to us. It may sometimes be greater, sometimes less. Who among the saints does not know the truth of this? With what life, what light, what strength does God's love appear to us at times! And at other times how dead, how dark, how weak his love appears to be! All the graces of the Spirit in us, all sanctified enjoyments whatever, are fruits of his love. How variously these fruits are brought to us! How differently, at different times and seasons to the same person, his love is felt, experience will abundantly testify.

(2) God 'pours out his love in our hearts by the Holy Spirit' (*Rom. 5:5*). The Holy Spirit gives us a sense of it. He makes it known to us. Now this varies and is changeable. Sometimes it is more, sometimes less. Now he shines, and now he hides his face. But it is all done for our good. Our Father will not always chide in case we are cast down. He does not always smile in case we take his love for granted and neglect him. But still his love is always the same. When for a while he hides his face, he still gathers us with everlasting kindness.

Objection. But you will say, 'This comes near to blasphemy! You are saying that God loves his people in their sinning as well as in their strictest obedience. If this is so, who will bother to serve him or seek to please him?'

Answer. There are few truths of Christ which have not been greatly misunderstood and twisted by the ignorance of foolish men. The love of God in itself is the eternal purpose and act of God's will. This is no more changeable than God himself. If it were, nobody could be saved. But God's love does not change and therefore we are not consumed in his wrath. Does God then love his people while they are sinning? Yes! he loves his people but he does not love their sinning. Doesn't God's love change towards them? Not the purpose of his will to love them, but the working out of his gracious acts and disciplines towards them is changed. He rebukes them, disciplines them, hides his face from them, smites them, fills them with a sense of his indignation, but woe to us if he should change his love, or take away his kindness from us! Those very things which seem to suggest that his love to us changes in fact come to us from his love to us. 'But won't this encourage sin?'. To suggest such a thing is to admit you have never tasted the love of God. The *doctrine* of grace may be turned into an excuse for doing evil but the *principle* cannot. And we may further affirm that God's detesting and loathing sin in his people is not inconsistent with the acceptance of their persons and their being chosen for eternal life.

Our love to God ebbs and flows, waxes and wanes, increases and decreases. We lose our first love, and we grow again in love. Unlike Christ, we are never the same yesterday, today and for ever. What poor creatures we are! How unlike the Lord and his love! Like Reuben, we are 'unstable as water and so cannot excel'. One moment we appear to stand. Like Peter we say, 'Though all men forsake you, I will not!'. Then we fall and deny Christ. One day we say, 'I shall never be moved, my hill is so strong'. The next we say, 'All men are liars, I shall perish'.

So we see how like and how unlike are our love to the Father and his love to us.

4: *Conclusions arising from the Doctrine of Communion with the Father in Love*

Having a loving fellowship with the Father is very much neglected by Christians. Ignorance of our mercies and our privileges is our sin as well as the cause of our troubles. We do not listen to the voice of the Spirit, 'that we may know the things that are freely given to us by God'. This makes Christians sad when they might be rejoicing. It makes them weak when they could be strong. How few Christians are actually acquainted with this great privilege of having a loving fellowship with the Father! How full of fears and doubts they are over his goodwill and kindness! At the best, many think that there is no good-will of the Father to us except that which was purchased at the high price of the blood of Jesus. It is true that only through Christ can we have any communion with the Father. But in fact, the free source of all desire for communion with us in the Godhead is in the heart of the Father. 'Eternal life was with the Father and is manifested to us.'

Let us then see the Father as full of love to us. Do not see the Father as one who is angry, but as one who is most kind and gentle. Let us see the Father as one who from eternity has always had kind thoughts towards us. It is a complete misunderstanding of the Father that makes us want to run away and hide from him. The Psalmist said, 'They that know you will put their trust in you.' How sad that we cannot stay long with God in spiritual meditations! The Father loses the company of his people because they are so ignorant of his love to them. His saints keep thinking only of his terrible majesty, severity and greatness, and so their hearts are not drawn to him in love. We must learn to think of his everlasting gentleness and compassion. We must remember his kind thoughts towards us which have been from eternity. Let us remember how eager and willing he is to accept us. If we did this, then we would not be able to bear one hour's absence from him. Instead, we find it difficult to spend even one hour with him. Let then this be the first thought that we have of the Father, that he is full of eternal love to us. Let our hearts and thoughts be filled with his love to us, even though many discouragements may lie in our way.

To raise our hearts to such thoughts of the Father, let us consider the following.

Consider who it is who loves us. It is the love of him who is in himself all-sufficient and who is infinitely satisfied with himself and his own glorious excellences and perfections. It is the love of him who has no need to seek the love of others for himself and no need to make himself happy by loving his creatures. He could, if he so wished, have rested with delight and satisfaction for all eternity in the happiness of his own self-sufficiency. He had his only-begotten Son also, his eternal wisdom to rejoice in and delight in from all eternity (*Prov. 8:30*). His only Son, by himself alone, would be sufficient to satisfy and delight the Father. But in spite of all this, the Father will love his saints also. And the Father's love is such that he does not seek his own happiness and satisfaction only, but ours also. It is the love of a God, the love of a Father whose character is kind and generous.

Consider what kind of love is the Father's love. The love of the Father is eternal. He loved us from before the foundation of the world. Before we ever existed or had done the least good, he thought of us and loved us and delighted in us. It was then, before the foundation of the world, that the Son of God rejoiced at fulfilling his Father's delight in him (*Prov. 8:30*). The delight of the Father in the Son, mentioned in this

[28]

verse, is not so much his absolute delight in him as the express image of his person and the brightness of his glory, in whom the Father might see reflected all his own excellences and perfections, but rather his love and delight in the sons of men. The order of the words leads to this conclusion. 'I was daily his delight' and 'my delights were with the sons of men.' By this the Son declares the thoughts of kindness and redemption he had for the sons of men. So the Father delighted in the Son for this very reason, that through his Son, his purpose to redeem and to show kindness to the sons of men would be shown. It was from eternity that the Father purposed in his heart to bring us to eternal happiness. The very thought of this is enough to make all that is within us, like the babe in Elizabeth's womb, leap for joy. An awareness of this loving, eternal purpose of the Father cannot but bring our souls to the lowest depths of a humble, holy reverence and to rejoice before God with trembling.

The love of the Father is freely given to us. He loves us because he wanted to love us. There was, there is, nothing in us to give God any reason why he should love us. If we deserved God's love, we would not value it so highly. Things which are owed to us are seldom gratefully received. But that which was in eternity before we existed, must of necessity be absolutely free if it is given to us for our well-being. This free choice of the Father as to whom he would love, and that he would love them, gives life and being to his love. It also gives the reason why he loves and gives value to his love (*Rom. 9:11; Eph. 1:3, 4; Tit. 3:5; James 1:18*).

The love of the Father is unchangeable. Though we change every day, yet his love does not change. If anything in us or on our part could stop God loving us, then he would long ago have turned away from us. It is because his love is fixed and unchangeable that the Father shows us infinite patience and forbearance. If his love was not unchangeable, we would perish (*II Pet. 3:9*).

The love of the Father is selective. God has not chosen to love everyone in the world. He says, 'Jacob have I loved, but Esau have I hated'. Why should the Father choose to love us and pass by millions who are no different from us? Why should God bring us to share in his love and all the wonderful things his love brings to us and shut out from his love the great and wise men of the world?

Let us, then, frequently consider these things and let the consideration of these things lead us to commune more and more with our loving heavenly Father.

You must, then, so believe as to receive the love of the Father. You do not hold communion with God in anything until you receive it by faith. You need to believe that God loves you, that his heart is filled with love to you and accept his word for it. You will never experience the sweetness of his love until you receive it. You must, then, continually remind yourself that God loves you and embraces you with his free eternal love. When the Lord is, by his Word, presented as a Father who loves you, then think about it and accept it. Then embrace him by faith and let your heart be filled with his love. Set your whole heart to receive his love and let your heart be bound with the cords of this love.

Let the love of the Father stir you to love him also. Then you will walk in the light of God's face and have holy communion with your Father all the day long. Do not treat him unkindly when he deals so kindly with you. Do not show such ingratitude to him who is your loving heavenly Father.

To stimulate you in this duty and the daily, constant practice of it, I will give you further important things to consider.

Consider that it is the greatest desire of God the Father that you should have loving fellowship with him. His greatest desire is that you should receive him into your soul as one full of love, tenderness and kindness to you. Flesh and blood is apt to think hard thoughts of God, to think that he is always angry and incapable of being pleased with his sinful creatures, that it is not for them to draw near to him, and that there is nothing in the world more to be desired than never to come into his presence. 'Who among us shall dwell with the devouring fire? Who among us shall dwell with everlasting burnings?' say sinners in Zion. 'I knew that you were a hard man', said the evil servant in the gospel. Now, there is nothing more grievous to the Lord, nothing that serves the purposes of Satan more than such thoughts as these. Satan rejoices when he can fill your heart with such hard thoughts of God. Satan's purpose from the beginning was to fill mankind with lies about God. The first blood that murderer shed was by this means. He led our first parents into hard thoughts about God. 'Has God said so? Has he threatened you with death? He knows well enough that if you eat of this fruit, it will be much better for you.' With these lies he succeeded in overthrowing all mankind at once. And remembering this great victory, he readily uses the same method with us. Now it is exceedingly grievous to the Spirit of God to be so slandered in the hearts of those whom he dearly loves. How he remonstrates with his people. 'What iniquity have you seen in me?', he asks. 'Have I been a wilderness to you, or a land of darkness?'. But Zion said, 'The Lord has forsaken me, and my Lord has forgotten me'. And see the Lord's reply: 'Can a woman forget her nursing child, and not have compassion on the son of her womb? Surely they may forget, yet I will not forget you' (*Isa. 49:14–16*).

The Father knows that his people can bring no greater hurt to his loving heart than to have such hard thoughts of him. He knows full well what fruits this bitter root is likely to bear. He

[31]

knows what alienations of heart, what drawing back, what unbelief this bitter root will bring forth. And worst of all, he knows how it leads us to avoid walking with him. How unwilling is a child to come into the presence of an angry father! Consider, then, that receiving the Father as one who loves us gives him the honour he desires and is exceedingly pleasing to him. Scripture sets out his love in a noteworthy way. 'He commends his love towards us' (*Rom. 5:8*). 'Behold what manner of love the Father has bestowed on us' (*I John 3:1*). Why, then, this foolishness? Why are we afraid to have good thoughts of God? Is it too hard to think of God as good, gracious, tender, loving and kind? I speak of saints. How easy we find it to think of God as hard, austere, severe, unable to be pleased and fierce, which are the very worst characteristics of men and therefore the most hated by God (*Rom. 1:31; II Tim. 3:3*). How easily Satan deceives us! Was it not his purpose from the beginning to inject such thoughts of God into our hearts? Assure yourself, then, that there is nothing more acceptable to the Father than for us to keep our hearts filled with him as the eternal source of all that rich grace which flows out to sinners in the blood of Jesus.

Many saints have no greater burden in their lives than that their hearts do not constantly delight and rejoice in God. There is still in them a resistance to walking close with God. Why is this? Is it not because they are not skilful and so neglect having loving fellowship with the Father? But the more we see of God's love, so much more shall we delight in him. All that we learn of God will only frighten us away from him if we do not see him as loving and merciful to us. But if your heart is taken up with the Father's love as the chief property of his nature, it cannot help but choose to be overpowered, conquered and embraced by him. This, if anything, will arouse our desire to make our eternal home with God. If the love of a father will not make a child delight in him, what will? So do this: set your thoughts on the eternal love of the Father and see if your heart is not aroused to delight in him. Sit down for a while at this delightful spring of living water and you will soon find its streams sweet and delightful. You who used to run from God will not now be able, even for a second, to keep at any distance from him.

Objection. But some may say, 'How is it possible to hold communion with the Father in love? I do not know whether he loves me or not. And how can I then dare to cast myself on his love? What if I am not accepted? Will I not perish for my presumption? God seems to me to be only a consuming fire and everlasting burnings. I am afraid to come close to him.'

Answer. Although the love of God is known by spiritual sense and experience, it is received only by faith. And the foundation of our knowing that God loves us is our receiving it by faith, because it has been revealed. 'We have known and believed the love that God has to us. God is love' (*I John 4:16*). This is the assurance which, at the very start of our walk with God, you may have of God's love. God, who is truth, has said it. Whatever your heart says, or Satan says, unless you believe the love God has to you, you make him a liar (*I John 5:10*).

Objection. 'I can believe that God is love to others, for he has told us that he is love. But that he loves me I find it hard to believe. There is no reason in the world, and nothing in me to cause God to think one loving, kind thought towards me. And therefore I dare not trust myself to his love. I dare not hold communion with God in his special love.'

Answer. God has spoken it to you in particular, in the same way that he has spoken it to anyone in the world. Nobody from the foundation of the world who believed such love in the Father, and made returns of love to him again, was ever deceived. Neither shall anyone, in so doing, be deceived by the Father to the end of the world. You have, then, a sure foundation. If you believe and receive the Father as love, he will infallibly be so to you, even though others may fall under his severity.

Objection. 'I cannot love God. If I found my soul loving God, I could then believe that he loved me.'

Answer. This is the most preposterous thing that could be said. It truly robs God of his glory. 'Herein is love,' says the Holy Spirit, 'not that we loved God, but that he loved us' (*I John 4:10, 11*). Note well that he loved us first. Would you then turn this upside down and say, 'In this is love, not that God loved me, but that I first loved him'? This is to take the glory of God away from him. God loves us when there is nothing in us to deserve his love or to cause him to love us. On the other hand, we have every reason in the world to love him. But you would have it the other way round. You would have it that there should be something in you for which God should love you. You would have it that God should love you because you first loved him. And you think you should love God before you see anything lovely in him. You first want to find out whether he loves you or not, before you love him. This is the way of the corrupt unbeliever. He will not believe until he first finds out. But that way will not bring glory to God nor peace to your soul. So lay aside your sinful doubts. Believe the Father loves you and open your soul to the Lord in loving fellowship with him.

Consider what a wonderful privilege has been given to the saints of God. This is the most wonderful privilege God could give to any of his creatures. Whatever the world may think of Christians, yet Christians have food to eat that the world knows nothing of. The saints have close communion and fellowship with the Father. Their relationship with the Father is a relationship of love. Men are generally esteemed by the company they keep. It is an honour to stand in the presence of princes, even if it be as a servant. What honour, then, have all the saints, to stand with boldness in the presence of the Father and there to enjoy his love! What a blessing did the Queen of Sheba pronounce on the servants of Solomon who stood before him and heard his wisdom. But how much more blessed are they who stand continually before the God of Solomon, hearing his wisdom and enjoying his love! Whilst others have their fellowship with Satan and with their own lusts, Christians have this sweet communion with the Father for ever.

And what a safe place the saints have to retreat to when they suffer the scorn, reproaches, scandals and misrepresentations of the world. When a child is bullied and hurt in the streets by strangers, he quickly runs home to the love and protection of his father. There he tells everything and is comforted. In all the hard words and slanders which the saints meet with in the streets of the world, they may come home to their Father and tell him all their troubles and sorrows and be comforted. 'As one whom his mother comforts, so will I comfort you,' says the Lord (*Isa. 66:13*). And the soul may say, 'If I am hated in the world, I will go where I know I am loved. Though all others hate me, yet my Father is tender and full of compassion. I will go to him and find happiness in him. In the world I am considered vile. I am frowned on and rejected. But I have honour and love with the Father whose kindness is better than life itself. There I shall have all things in their fulness, which others have only in dribs and drabs. There is in my Father's love everything I desire. There I find the sweetness of all his infinite mercies.'

It is clear, then, that Christians are the most misunderstood people in the world. If Christians say, 'Come and have fellowship with us,' the world is ready to retort, 'Have fellowship with you! Who are you? You are a company of foolish people. We despise your fellowship. When we intend to leave fellowship with all honest men and with men who are worth knowing, then we will come to you.' But how sadly mistaken is the world! Truly the fellowship with Christians is with the Father. Let the world think as they please, but Christians have intimate, spiritual, heavenly joys, because their fellowship is a fellowship of love with the Father. Christians are looked on as poor, low, despicable persons, when indeed they are the only great and noble persons in the world (*II Cor. 6:8–10*). Consider the company Christians keep. It is with the Father of glory. So Christians are indeed the excellent in the earth (*Psa. 16:3*).

This also shows clearly the difference between true and false Christians. Outwardly, both do the same things and enjoy the same privileges. But now enter into their secret prayers and thoughts. What a difference there is! There the saints hold communion with God. Hypocrites for the most part commune with the world and with their own lusts. They listen to what their lusts have to say, and then they make provision for them. The saints, on the other hand, are sweetly wrapped up in the love of their Father. Often it is impossible that believers should be better outwardly than those with rotten hearts. But this fellowship with the Father true Christians have, of which hypocrites know nothing. They have this feast in the Father's banqueting house, in which hypocrites have no share. In the multitude of their thoughts, the comforts of God their Father revive their souls.

Application. If these things be so, 'What sort of people ought we to be in our holy behaviour?'. 'Our God is a consuming fire.' 'What communion is there between light and darkness?'. Shall sin and lust dwell in those thoughts which receive from and give out love to the Father? Holiness is required in his presence for ever. An unclean spirit cannot draw near to God. An unholy heart cannot abide with God. A lewd person will not desire to hold fellowship with one who is pure. And will a man with vain and foolish thoughts hold

[36]

communion and dwell with the most holy God? Thinking much of the Father's love is a powerful motive to holiness and leads the soul into holiness. Ephraim says, 'What have I to do any more with idols?'. And when did he say it? When he found salvation in God. Communion with God is wholly inconsistent with loose walking (*I John 1:6; 2:4*). The one who claims to have fellowship with the Father and who does not keep his commandments is a liar. The love of the world and of the Father cannot dwell together.

How many who call themselves Christians come short of the reality! How ignorant are so many Christians of the mystery of this communion of love with the Father. How many hold communion with their lusts and with the world, and yet are considered to be great Christians. They have no new name, no white stone of reality, and yet many call them the people of God. Far from having communion with God, the reality is that God is not in all their thoughts. May the Lord open their eyes that they may see and know that walking with God is a matter, not of the outward appearance, but of the inward reality.

5: *Fellowship with Jesus Christ, the Son of God*

The fellowship which the saints have with the Son of God, Jesus Christ our Lord, is fellowship with him as Mediator. Into this office of Mediator Christ submitted himself for our sakes, 'being born of a woman, born under the law, to redeem those who were under the law, that we might receive the adoption of sons' (*Gal. 4:4, 5*).

Scripture shows that Christians have such fellowship with Jesus Christ (*I Cor. 1:9*). This is that fellowship to which all saints are called, and in which, by the faithfulness of God, they shall be kept. We are called by God the Father, who loves us, to this fellowship with his Son our Lord.

Jesus says, 'Behold I stand at the door and knock. If anyone hears my voice and opens the door, I will come in to him and dine with him, and he with me' (*Rev. 3:20*). If this is not fellowship, then I do not know what fellowship is. Christ will dine with believers. Christ refreshes himself with his own graces in his people, by his Spirit which he has given them. The Lord Christ greatly delights in the sweet fruits of the Spirit in his saints. An example of this is given in the Song of Solomon, where the Shulamite prays that she may have something to entertain her beloved when he comes to her (*Song 4:16*). The souls of the saints are the garden of Jesus Christ, that good ground which is blessed by God (*Heb. 6:7*). Christ rejoices in the souls of his saints (*Prov. 8:31*). He 'rejoices over them' (*Zeph. 3:17*). The souls of Christ's people are a garden for fruit, pleasant fruit (*Song 4:12–14*). Whatever is sweet and delicious, whatever is pleasant and sweet to the smell, whatever is useful and good for medicine,

[38]

is in this garden. There are all sorts of spiritual things in the souls of the saints for the Lord Jesus. It is for this reason that the Shulamite is so earnest in her prayer that these things may be so increased in her that her beloved may dine with her as he has promised. 'O that the yearnings and worship of the Spirit of all grace might stir up all his gifts and graces in me, so that the Lord Jesus, the beloved of my soul, may be well entertained and pleased when he comes to have fellowship with me.'

God complains of lack of fruit in his vineyard (*Isa. 5:2; Hos. 10:1*). Lack of good food for her beloved's entertainment is what the Shulamite feared, and desired to prevent. A barren heart is not fit to receive Christ. So how can we allow our hearts to be barren and unfit for him, when we know what unspeakable delight he takes in the fruit of the Spirit? Moreover, as Christ dines with his saints, so he has promised that they shall dine with him. Christ provides for their entertainment in a most wonderful way (*Prov. 9:2*). Christ calls the good things that he has for them a 'feast', a 'wedding', a 'feast of fat things with good wine'. The fatted calf is killed for their entertainment. Such is the communion and such is the mutual entertainment of Christ and his saints in that communion.

The beloved says, 'I am the rose of Sharon, and the lily of the valleys' (*Song 2:1*). The Lord Christ is compared to all that is most glorious and beautiful in his creation. He is, in the heavens, as glorious as the sun, and as the bright morning star. Among the beasts he is like the lion, the lion of the tribe of Judah. Among the flowers, Christ is as beautiful and as glorious as the rose and the lily. He is like the rose for the sweetness of its perfume, and like the lily for its beauty. Solomon in all his glory was not arrayed like one of these. But Christ is more than an ordinary rose. He is the 'rose of Sharon'. Sharon was a fruitful plain where the best herds were fed (*I Chron. 27:29*). The plain of Sharon was so beautiful and so fruitful that it is promised to the church that there shall be given to it the glory of Sharon (*Isa. 35:2*). This fruitful plain, no doubt, grew the most precious roses. Christ, in the beauty of his love, and in his righteousness, is like this excellent rose, drawing the hearts of his saints to him. As God smelled a soothing aroma from the blood of Christ's atonement, so from the graces with which he is anointed by God for his people, his saints receive a refreshing, lovely scent of a soothing aroma. The scent of a soothing aroma symbolises all that is acceptable and delightful (*Gen. 8:21*).

Christ is also 'the lily of the valleys'. Of all flowers, this is the most beautiful (*Matt. 6:29*). So Christ is most desirable for the beauty and perfection of his person. He is incomparably fairer than the children of men. Christ, who is to his people one who abundantly satisfies all their spiritual senses, who is their refreshment, their beauty, their delight, their glory, goes on to tell his people what they are to him. 'Like a lily among thorns, so is my love among the daughters' (*Song 2:2*). Christ and his church are both described by the same object, the lily, showing that their union is by the same indwelling Spirit and that his saints are conformed to his image and likeness, to which they were predestined (*Rom. 8:29*). The church, like a lily, is very beautiful to Christ.

The church is like 'the lily among thorns', because Christ's people excel all others. As the lily excels thorns, so in Christ's eyes believers in him excel all unbelievers.

The church is like 'the lily among thorns', because the church is faithful and keeps her beauty under sore trials. The world is described as being 'pricking briers and painful thorns to the house of Israel' (*Ezek. 28:24*). 'The best of them is like a brier; the most upright is sharper than a thorn hedge' (*Mic. 7:4*). So we see what Christ is to his people, and what he is to the church.

And now we see what Christ is in the church's estimation. 'Like an apple tree among the trees of the wood, so is my beloved among the sons. I sat down in his shade with great delight, and his fruit was sweet to my taste' (*Song 2:3*).

The Shulamite begins to speak her thoughts. She shows her delight in her beloved. So the church delights in her beloved, Christ. As Christ compares the church to a lily among thorns, so she compares Christ to the apple tree among the trees of the wood, because the apple tree has two things other trees do not have. The apple tree has fruit for food and shade for comfort. She eats its fruit and rests in its shade, and she does both with great delight. So the church feeds on Christ and rests in the shade of his love.

'So is my beloved among the sons.' All other sons, whether angels, the sons of God by creation, or the sons of Abraham, the best of his offspring, or the sons of the old creation, however high they are in the world's esteem, are to a hungry weary soul – for only such seek shade and fruit – like the fruitless, leafless trees of the forest which give neither fruit nor shade. 'In Christ,' says the church, 'there is fruit, sweet-tasting fruit. His flesh is food indeed and his blood is drink indeed' (*John 6:55*). Moreover, Christ has brought that everlasting righteousness which will abundantly satisfy any hungry soul after that hungry soul has gone to many a barren tree for food and found none. Christ abounds in precious and pleasant graces, which I may take and eat. In fact, he calls me to eat and to go on eating until I am full. These are the fruits which Christ bears. He is the tree that produces everything necessary for life. Christ is that tree of life which has produced everything that is necessary for eternal life. In Christ is that righteousness for which we hunger. In Christ is that water of life of which whoever drinks shall never thirst again. Oh, how sweet are the fruits of Christ's mediation to the faith of his saints! He that can find no mercy, pardon, grace, acceptance with God, holiness, sanctification and all other things necessary for salvation is an utter stranger to these things which are prepared for believers only.

Christ also is a shade giving comfort and shelter. He shelters from outward wrath, and gives comfort for inner weariness. The first use of the shade is to protect us from the heat of the sun, as did Jonah's gourd. When the heat of God's wrath is ready to scorch the soul, Christ shades the soul from its heat. Under the shadow of his wings we sit down quietly, safely, because we put our trust in him. And all this we do with great delight. Who can describe the joy of a soul safely sheltered from wrath by the covering of the righteousness of the Lord Jesus? There is also comfort in shade from weariness. Christ is 'as the shadow of a great rock in a weary land' (*Isa. 32:2*). From the power of corruptions, the trouble of temptations, the distress of persecutions, there is in Christ quiet, rest and peace (*Matt. 11:27, 28*).

Having described each other, and so made it clear that they cannot but be delighted in that fellowship and communion they have with each other, the Shulamite goes on to describe more fully that fellowship, and from her description we can learn the delights of fellowship between Christ and his people.

'He brought me to the banqueting house, and his banner over me was love. Sustain me with cakes and raisins, refresh me with apples, for I am lovesick. His left hand is under my head, and his right hand embraces me' (*Song 2:4–6*).

This fellowship is like a delicious banquet. 'He brought me to the banqueting house' or 'house of wine'. This fellowship is described under images of the greatest sweetness and most delicious refreshment. 'He entertains me,' says the Shulamite, 'as if I was some great person'. Great persons, at great entertainments, are brought into the banqueting house, the house of wine and excellent food. These are the provisions of grace and mercy, love and kindness, and everything that is promised in the gospel, preached in the assemblies of the saints, and revealed by the Spirit. This 'love is better than wine' (*Song 1:2*). It is 'not food and drink, but righteousness, peace and joy in the Holy Spirit'. Gospel promises are delicious morsels. Whether these houses symbolise the Scriptures, the gospel or the ordinances, or any wonderful revelation of special love, as banqueting is not done every day, nor used in ordinary entertaining, it does not matter. Wine that cheers the heart of man, that makes him forget his misery, that gives him a cheerful appearance is that which is promised (*Prov. 31:6, 7; Gal. 4:9, 12*). The grace shown by Christ in his ordinances is refreshing, strengthening and full of comfort to the souls of the saints. Woe to such souls who loathe these honeycombs! But in this way, Christ makes all his assemblies banqueting houses. There he gives his saints rich entertainment.

This fellowship is delightful. 'Sustain me with cakes of raisins, refresh me with apples, for I am lovesick.' The Shulamite is quite overwhelmed with the richness of the entertainment. So Christ's people find love, care and kindness poured out by Christ in the assemblies of the saints.

When the soul discovers the excellency and sweetness of Christ in the banqueting house, it is overcome and cries out to be made partaker of his fulness. The soul is 'lovesick' – overcome with the mighty power of God's love. Having once tasted the sweetness of Christ in the banqueting house, and not being fully satisfied, makes the heart sick. Therefore the soul cries out, 'Sustain me. I have caught a glimpse of the King in his beauty! I have tasted the fruit of his righteousness. My soul longs for him. Oh, support and sustain my spirit with his presence in his ordinances or I shall sink down and faint. Oh, what have you done, blessed Jesus! I have seen you and my soul is overwhelmed with your love. Let me have something from you to support me, or I die.'

When a person is fainting, two things are needed to help him. Strength is to be used to stop him falling to the ground, and inward comfort is needed to refresh and revive his fainting spirit. For these two things the soul prays – overcome and fainting with the strength of its own love and raised by a sense of Christ's love. The fainting soul desires strengthening grace to support it so that it may be able to attend to its duty. The soul also desires the comforts of the Holy Spirit to revive it and to satisfy it until it comes to a full enjoyment of Christ.

This fellowship is a fellowship in which the soul finds safety and protection. 'His banner over me was love.' The banner is a symbol of safety and protection, a sign that the host was present. Those who belonged to an army camp stood under their banner for security. Every tribe of the children of Israel, whilst in the wilderness, encamped under its own banner. A banner is also a symbol of success and victory (*Psa. 20:5*). Christ has a banner for his saints, and that banner is love. All their protection is from his love, and they shall have all the protection his love can give them. This keeps them safe from hell, death and all the threats of their enemies. Whoever or whatever would try and get at Christ's people to hurt them must pass through the banner of the love of the Lord Jesus. Christ's people, then, have great spiritual safety and this is another wonderful thing about communion with the Lord Jesus.

This fellowship is a fellowship in which the soul finds strength and comfort. 'His left hand is under my head, and his right hand embraces me.' Christ is here seen as a kind friend to anyone who is sick or sad. The soul faints with love. The soul has spiritual desires for the enjoyment of Christ's presence. And Christ comes to the soul with his loving embrace. He nourishes and cherishes his church (*Eph. 5:29; Isa. 63:9*). Now 'the hand under the head' symbolises supporting, upholding grace in trial and difficulties. And 'the hand that embraces' is the hand upon the heart, bringing joy and comfort. In both these, Christ is seen rejoicing as 'the bridegroom rejoices over the bride' (*Isa. 62:5*). Now to lie in the arms of Christ's love, supported and comforted by him is constantly to hold communion with him. So the Shulamite says, 'I charge you, O daughters of Jerusalem, by the gazelles or by the does of the field, do not stir up nor awaken love until it pleases' (*Song 2:7*). She is most earnest that this fellowship should not be disturbed, charging all so to behave that her beloved is not provoked to depart. So the church also prays that nothing should disturb fellowship with Christ and provoke him to depart.

This whole book called 'The Song of Solomon' describes the communion between the Lord Christ and his saints. Therefore it is needless to take any more illustrations from it. I shall only add that of Proverbs 9:1–5.

The Lord Christ, the eternal wisdom of the Father, who makes him wisdom to us, sets up a spiritual house in which he makes provision for the entertainment of those guests whom he so freely invites. His church is the house which he has built on a perfect number of pillars so that it might be stable, resting on a good foundation. His slain beasts and mixed wine with which his table is spread are those spiritual, fat things of the gospel which he has so graciously prepared for those that come in answer to his invitation. Surely to eat of this bread and to drink of this wine is to hold fellowship with the Lord Jesus Christ, the eternal Son of God.

6: *Fellowship with Christ in Grace*

Grace is everywhere in Scripture ascribed to Jesus as his chief characteristic. He dwelt among us, 'full of grace and truth' (*John 1:14*). All who were before Christ were but symbols and representatives of grace. Only by Christ did grace come in truth and reality. 'Grace and truth came by Jesus Christ' (*John 1:17*). 'And of his fulness have we all received and grace for grace' (*John 1:16*). That is, we have communion with Christ in grace. We receive from Jesus all manner of grace whatever. In grace, then, we have fellowship with Jesus.

In the apostolic blessing, grace is also ascribed to our Lord Jesus Christ (*II Cor 13:14*). Paul is so delighted with this that he makes it his motto (*II Thess. 3:17, 18*). Paul makes these two – 'Grace be with you' and 'The Lord Jesus be with you' – equivalent expressions. Grace, then, is that which we are especially to see in the Lord Jesus. Grace is that which we are to receive from him. That grace which is revealed in the gospel is that grace by which we have fellowship with Jesus Christ. Christ is the headstone in the building of the temple of God, to whom 'grace, grace' is to be shouted (*Zech. 4:7*).

Grace is a word which has various meanings. But chiefly it means three things:

(1) Grace can mean grace of personal presence and beauty. So we say, 'He or she is a graceful and beautiful person'. The Song of Solomon deals mainly with the grace and beauty of Christ's person. See also Psalm 45:2.

(2) Grace can mean grace of free favour and acceptance. 'By grace you are saved'. That is, we are saved by the free favour and merciful acceptance of God in Christ. So the

expression 'If I have found grace in your sight' is often used. The person using this expression hopes that he will be freely and favourably accepted. So God 'gives grace', that is, favour, to the humble (*James 4:6; Gen. 39:21; 41:37; Acts 7:10; I Sam. 2:26; II Kings 25:27*).

(3) Grace can mean the fruit of the Spirit sanctifying and renewing our natures, enabling us to do those good things which God has purposed and planned for us to do, and holding us back from evil. 'My grace is sufficient for you,' says the Lord Christ. That is, the help which God gave was sufficient for Paul (*II Cor. 12:9; 8:6, 7; Col. 3:16; Heb. 12:28*).

The last two meanings of the word grace, as relating to Christ, I call 'purchased grace', being purchased by him for us. And our communion with Jesus in this purchased grace is called 'a fellowship in his sufferings, and the power of his resurrection' (*Phil. 3:10*).

Let us, then, begin with the first meaning and use of the word grace, which I call 'personal grace'.

The personal grace of Christ refers to him as Mediator. Therefore by the grace of Christ's person I do not mean the glorious excellences of his deity as separate from the office of Mediator, which for us as the God-man he undertook. Nor do I mean the outward appearance of his human nature, either as he lived here on earth or as exalted in heaven, which is but 'to know Christ after the flesh' (*II Cor. 5:16*). But what I mean to show are the graces of the person of Christ as Mediator. I intend to show his spiritual glory and beauty, as appointed and anointed by the Father to the great work of bringing home all his elect.

In this respect, Scripture describes Christ as exceedingly excellent, beautiful and desirable. As Mediator, as God and man in the same person, Christ cannot be compared with the greatest created good (*Psa. 45:2*). Christ is beyond comparison. He is more beautiful and gracious than anything here on earth. The prophet Isaiah, calling the Messiah 'the branch of the Lord' and 'the fruit of the earth', declares that Christ shall be 'beautiful and glorious, excellent and appealing' (*Isa. 4:2*). And Paul says, 'in him dwells all the fulness of the Godhead bodily' (*Col. 2:9*).

When the Shulamite is asked about the personal excellences of her beloved, she says, 'My beloved is white and ruddy, chief among ten thousand' (*Song 5:10*). Then she proceeds to describe him by his personal excellences to the end of the chapter, concluding with the statement that 'he is altogether lovely' (*v. 16*). But she particularly describes him as 'white and ruddy', that is, of beautiful complexion.

He is white in the glory of his deity and ruddy in the preciousness of his humanity. Jacob, describing Shiloh or the Messiah, says, 'His eyes are darker than wine, and his teeth whiter than milk' (*Gen. 49:12*). Whiteness is the complexion of glory (*Dan. 7:9; Matt. 17:2; Mark 9:3; Rev. 1:14*). The angels and glorified saints that always behold him, and who are fully changed into the image of the same glory, are said to be in white robes. So his whiteness is his deity and the glory of his deity.

He is also ruddy in the beauty of his humanity. Man was called Adam from the red earth from which he was made. The word used here points Christ out as the second Adam, partaker of flesh and blood, because the children also partook of the same (*Heb. 2:14*). The beauty and glory of the Lord Jesus is seen in the union of both these natures in one person.

Christ is also white in the beauty of his innocence and holiness, and ruddy in the blood of his sacrifice. Whiteness is the badge of innocence and holiness. It is said of the Nazarites, who were symbols of holiness, that 'they were brighter than snow, they were whiter than milk' (*Lam. 4:7*). And Isaiah shows that scarlet, red and crimson are the colours of sin and guilt, and white the colour of innocence (*Isa. 1:18*). Christ was 'a lamb without blemish and without spot' (*I Pet. 1:19*). He 'committed no sin, nor was guile found in his mouth' (*I Pet. 2:22*). He was 'holy, harmless, undefiled, separate from sinners' (*Heb. 7:26*). Yet he who was so white in his innocence was made ruddy in his own blood.

He was made ruddy in the pouring out of his blood, his precious blood, in that agony of his soul, when thick drops of blood trickled to the ground (*Luke 22:44*).

He was made ruddy also when the whips and thorns, nails and spears caused him to bleed profusely (*John 19:34*). Christ was made ruddy by being drenched all over in his own blood.

He was made ruddy by the imputation of sin, whose colour is red and crimson (*II Cor. 5:21*). He who was white became ruddy for our sakes, pouring out his blood as an offering for sin. By his whiteness he fulfilled the law. By his redness he satisfied justice.

As King, Christ is white and ruddy. He is white in love and mercy to his own people. He is red with justice and revenge towards his enemies (*Isa. 63:3; Rev. 19:13*).

THE PERSONAL EXCELLENCE AND GRACE OF THE LORD JESUS CHRIST IS SEEN IN THE GRACE OF UNION AND THE GRACE OF COMMUNION

By the grace of union, Christ is fit to save. The uniting of the nature of God and the nature of man in one person made Christ fit to be a Saviour to the utmost. He lays his hand upon God by partaking of his nature (*Zech. 13:7*). And he lays his hand upon us, partaking of our nature (*Heb. 1:14, 16*). And so he becomes an umpire or referee between God and man, making sure each side fulfils its promises and obligations to the other. By this means, Christ brings God and man together who were driven apart by sin. We who were afar off are brought near to God by Christ. For this very reason, he had room enough in his heart to receive us and strength enough in his spirit to bear all the wrath that was prepared for us. Sin brought infinite punishment because it was committed against an infinite God. Christ, being the infinite God in human nature, could suffer the infinite punishment that the sinner deserved. And so, by this personal union in Christ we are saved.

By the grace of communion, Christ's fulness is able to save to the uttermost. 'Of his fulness we have all received, and grace for grace' (*John 1:16*). The results of this union come to us freely by grace. So Christ 'is able to save to the uttermost those who come to God through him' (*Heb. 7:25*). He is able to save to the uttermost because he received from the Father by the Spirit all that was necessary for the work of our salvation. For our salvation, all fulness was communicated to Christ, 'for it pleased the Father that in him all the fulness should dwell' (*Col. 1:19*). And Christ did not receive the 'Spirit by measure' (*John 3:34*). So from this fulness, Christ is all-sufficient to supply all the needs of his people (*John 1:16*). Had the Spirit been given to Christ by measure, we would soon have exhausted all his supplies. So because of his fulness, Christ has all sufficiency in himself to be to the soul all that the soul desires. Is the soul dead? Christ is its life. Is the soul weak? Christ is its strength. Is the soul ignorant? Christ is its wisdom. Is the soul guilty? Christ is its righteousness and justification.

Many poor creatures are aware of their needs, but do not know where to find the remedy. Indeed, whether it be life or light, power or joy, all is wrapped up in Christ.

So Christ is a fit Saviour, having pity and ability, gentleness and power, to carry on the work of salvation to the uttermost.

Christ is a full and complete Saviour, for he is made to us redemption, sanctification and righteousness, and he gives us his Spirit. Christ is also sufficient for all the needs of our souls. So he becomes exceedingly desirable and altogether lovely. It is in this that the saints have distinct fellowship with the Lord Christ.

Only Christ can satisfy the soul. All other ways and things will only end in disappointment.

In the Song of Solomon, the daughters of Jerusalem, symbolising common seekers after Christ, having heard the Shulamite describing her beloved, are stirred to seek him with her (*Song 5:10–16; 6:1*). What Paul says of those that crucified Christ may be said of all that reject him or refuse to have fellowship with him. Christ himself calls them 'simple ones', 'fools' and 'scorners' that despise his gracious invitation (*Prov. 1:22*). Only those who do not know Christ despise him. And they despise him because the god of this world has blinded their eyes so that they should not be able to see anything of his glory. The souls of men naturally seek something which will bring rest and peace of mind, something that will satisfy and delight them. There are two ways that men go about trying to get what they are looking for. Some set before themselves a certain aim. Some seek pleasure and others profit. In religion, acceptance with God is sought. Others seek some purpose in life, but without any certainty of finding it. They try one path, then another, and though weary with seeking and never finding, yet they refuse to give up. In whatever condition you may be, either in greediness, chasing after some futile secular or religious aim, or wandering about in your foolish imaginations, succeeding only in driving yourself to despair, compare what you are aiming at, or what you are doing, with what you have already heard of Jesus Christ. If what you are seeking is like Christ or equal to him, then reject Christ as one who has nothing desirable in him. But if you find that all your life is full of foolishness and troubles compared to Christ, why do you spend your 'money for that which is not bread, and your labour for that which does not satisfy'?

Now a word to you that are young, who are full of health and strength and who are chasing after some beloved ambition or some beloved pleasure. Stop and consider. What are all your beloveds compared to Christ the true beloved? What satisfaction and happiness have your beloveds brought you? Show us the peace, quietness and assurance of ever-lasting blessedness that they have brought you. Their paths are crooked. Whoever walks in them shall not know peace. So look and see that there is a fit object for your highest love, one in whom you may find rest to your soul, one in whom you will find nothing to grieve and trouble you to eternity. Behold, he stands at the door of your souls and knocks. Do not reject him, lest you seek for him and do not find him. Why do you spend your time in idleness and foolishness, wasting your precious time? Why associate with those who scoff at religion and the things of God? You only do this because you do not know the Lord Jesus Christ. When he reveals himself to you and tells you he is Jesus the Son of God whom you have slighted and refused, how it will break your hearts and fill you with sorrow and remorse because you have neglected him. If you never come to know him, then it would have been better if you had never been born. 'Today, if you hear his voice, do not harden your hearts.'

And a word now to you who are perhaps seeking earnestly for a righteousness by your own efforts and good works. Consider a little with yourselves. Is not Christ the only perfect righteousness, the only righteousness that will satisfy God? Why then trust in your own righteousness when God sent him to be your righteousness? Has Christ his rightful place in your hearts? Does he mean anything to you? Is he in all your thoughts? Do you know him in all his glory and beauty? Do you desire him more and more? Do you really count all things 'loss and dung' in comparison to him? Or do you prefer almost anything in the world to him? We shall talk more of this later.

7: *How Believers hold Communion with the Lord Jesus Christ in Grace*

Scripture shows us that we hold communion with the Lord Jesus in grace by a marriage relationship. Christ is married to us and we to him. This spiritual relation is accompanied with mutual love, and so in this fellowship with Christ we experience and enjoy all the excellent things which are in him.

This the Shulamite declares: 'My beloved is mine, and I am his' (*Song. 2:16*). He is mine. I possess him. I claim him as my head and my husband. I am his. He possesses me, owns me and has taken me into a personal marriage relationship with himself.

In Isaiah we read, 'Your Maker is your husband, the Lord of hosts is his name; and your Redeemer is the Holy One of Israel; he is called the God of the whole earth' (*Isa. 54:5*). This is given as the reason why the church will not be ashamed nor confounded in the midst of her trials and troubles. She is married to her Maker, and her Redeemer is her husband and so we see the mutual glory of Christ and his church walking together. 'I will greatly rejoice in the Lord, my soul shall be joyful in my God; for he has clothed me with the garments of salvation, he has covered me with the robe of righteousness, as a bridegroom decks himself with ornaments, and as a bride adorns herself with her jewels' (*Isa. 61:10*). As with couples on their wedding day, so it is with Christ and his saints. He is a husband to them.

Again, the Lord says, 'I will betroth you to me forever, yes, I will betroth you to me in righteousness and justice, in lovingkindness and mercy; I will betroth you to me in faithfulness, and you shall know the Lord' (*Hos. 2:19, 20*). So it is the main purpose of the gospel ministry to persuade men to give themselves to the Lord Christ as he reveals his kindness and willingness to be a husband to us. That is why Paul told the Corinthians, 'I have betrothed you to one husband, that I may present you as a chaste virgin to Christ' (*II Cor. 11:2*).

This is a relationship in which Christ delights and invites others to look at him in this his glory. 'Go forth,' he says, 'O daughters of Zion, and see King Solomon with the crown with which his mother crowned him on the day of his espousals, the day of the gladness of his heart' (*Song 3:11*). He calls to the daughters of Zion, who symbolise all sorts of professing Christians, to consider him in the condition of betrothing and espousing his church to himself. On account of this, Christ tells his people that they are to him both honour and delight.

Believers are an honour to Christ. It is the day of his coronation, and his spouse is the crown with which he is crowned. As Christ is 'a crown of glory and a diadem of beauty to the remnant of his people', so his church 'shall also be a crown of glory in the hand of the Lord, and a royal diadem in the hand of your God' (*Isa. 28:5; 62:3*). Christ makes this relationship with his saints to be his glory and honour.

Believers are a great delight to Christ. The day of his wedding, of taking poor sinful souls into his loving care, is the day of the gladness of his heart. John the Baptist was but a friend of the bridegroom, who stood and heard his voice when Christ was taking his bride to himself, and he rejoiced greatly (*John 3:29*). How much more, then, must be the joy and gladness of the bridegroom, as the prophet Zephaniah tells us: 'He will rejoice over you with gladness, he will rejoice over you with singing' (*Zeph. 3:17*).

It is the gladness of the heart of Christ, the joy of his soul, to take poor sinners into this relationship with himself. He rejoiced in the thoughts of it from eternity (*Prov. 8:31*). And how willing he was to undertake the hard task required to bring this relationship to reality (*Psa. 40:7, 8; Heb. 10:7*). He suffered the pangs of a woman in childbirth until he had accomplished this task (*Luke 12:50*). Because he loved his church, he gave himself for it (*Eph. 5:25*). He despised the shame and endured the cross (*Heb. 12:2*). He did all this that he might enjoy his bride, that he might be for her, and she for him, and not for another (*Hos. 3:3*). This is the joy he has when he is thus crowned by his mother. And who is his mother? It is believers who are mother and brother and sister to this Solomon (*Matt. 12:49, 50*). Believers crown him on his wedding day, giving themselves to him, and becoming his glory (*II Cor. 8:23*).

When Christ takes the church to himself, that is the day of his marriage and the church is his bride, his wife (*Rev. 19:7, 8*). The entertainment Christ makes for his saints is a wedding supper (*Matt. 22:3*). The graces of his church are the jewels of his queen (*Psa. 45:9–14*). And the fellowship Christ has with his saints is like that which a loving husband and wife have with each other. So Paul, in describing a human marriage, likens it to the marriage between Christ and his church (*Eph. 5:22–32*).

How we are to have communion with Christ in this marriage relationship. In this relationship, there are some things that are common both to Christ and to his saints, and some things that are special to each of them as the relationship requires.

In this relationship, there are two things of which we are especially to take note. We must take note that there is a mutual committal of each to the other in a marriage union, and there is a mutual love for each other arising from this union.

There is a mutual committing of each to the other in this marriage union. This is the first act of communion arising from the personal union with the grace of Christ. Christ commits himself to the soul, to love, care for and show kindness to it as a husband does to his wife. The soul, in response, gives itself up wholly to the Lord Christ to be to him a loving, tender, obedient wife. The prophet Hosea describes this in the relationship between himself and his unfaithful wife, Gomer (*Hos. 3:3*). 'Poor prostitutes,' says the Lord Christ, 'I have bought you for myself with the price of my own blood; and now this is the agreement we shall make with each other. I will be for you, and you shall be for me, and not for another.'

This relationship begins with Christ giving himself to the soul to be its Saviour, head and husband to dwell with that soul for ever. Christ looks with joy upon the souls of his saints. Christ loves their souls, sees them as fair and beautiful, because he has made them so (*Song 1:5; Ezek. 16:14*). Therefore he desires to enjoy fellowship with his spouse (*Song 2:14*). 'O my dove in the clefts of the rock, in the secret places of the cliff, let me see your countenance, let me hear your voice; for your voice is sweet, and your countenance is lovely.' As if to say, 'Do not hide yourself as one that flees to the clefts of the rocks. Do not be timid and fearful like one that hides in the secret places and is afraid to come out. Do not be cast down at the weakness of your prayers. Let me hear you sighing and groaning for me. They are sweet and delightful to my ears. Let me see your spiritual face seeking for and desiring heavenly things. A look from you brings great joy and delight to me.'

Nor does he leave her only with these words, but urges her to a closer union with himself. 'Come with me from Lebanon, my spouse, with me from Lebanon. Look from the top of Amana, from the top of Senir and Hermon, from the

[57]

lions' dens, from the mountains of the leopards' (*Song 4:8*). As if to say, 'You are in a wandering condition, like the Israelites of old, among sins and troubles which are lions and leopards to you. Come to me and I will give you peace and comfort' (*Matt. 11:28*). So the spouse boldly concludes that the desire of Christ is for her fellowship, that he does indeed love her and is determined to have her for himself (*Song 7:10*). So in carrying on this union, Christ freely gives himself to the soul. Precious and excellent as Christ is, he becomes ours. He makes himself available to us with all his graces. So the spouse says, 'My beloved is mine. In all that he is, Christ is mine. Because he is righteousness, he is the Lord my righteousness. Because he is the wisdom and power of God, he is made to me wisdom' (*Jer. 23:6; I Cor. 1:30*). So the 'Branch of the Lord is beautiful and glorious, and the fruit of the earth is excellent and appealing for those of Israel who have escaped' (*Isa. 4:2*). This is the first act of fellowship on Christ's part in this spiritual union between him and the believer. Christ gives himself freely to us to be our Christ, our beloved, to fulfil all the purposes of his love, mercy, grace and glory. Christ was set up to be the Mediator between God and his elect, and to enter into a marriage covenant with his people, a covenant that will never be broken.

The Lord Jesus Christ, then, was set up and prepared to be a husband to his saints, his church. He undertook the work of Mediator for which he was especially filled with the Spirit. As Mediator he purchased for his people grace and glory. Now he offers himself to them in the promises of the gospel, making himself desirable to them. He convinces them of his good will, and that he is sufficient for all their needs. And when they agree to receive him, which is all he requires or expects from them, he enters into a marriage contract to be theirs for ever.

[58]

On the saints' part, all that is required is their free, willing agreement to receive, embrace and submit to the Lord Jesus as Husband, Lord and Saviour, to abide with him, subject their souls to him to be ruled by him for ever.

This is the first act of union the soul makes with Christ. Following on this first act, there are renewed acts of receiving and embracing Christ all our days. It is in this latter sense that real communion with Christ lies.

The soul loves Christ for his beauty, grace and all-sufficiency. The soul sees Christ as far to be preferred above all other beloveds whatever (*Song 5:9*). To the soul, Christ is 'altogether lovely' (*Song 5:16*). He is infinitely more preferable than the highest, greatest good. The soul sees all that is of the world, 'the lust of the flesh, the lust of the eyes, and the pride of life,' and sees it all to be but vanity, for 'the world is passing away, and the lust of it' (*I John 2:16, 17*). These beloveds are in no way to be compared to Christ. The soul looks at legal righteousness, blamelessness with men, moral, upright behaviour, prompt obedience to duties, and says with Paul, 'I count all things loss for the excellence of the knowledge of Christ Jesus my Lord, for whom I have suffered the loss of all things, and count them as rubbish, that I may gain Christ' (*Phil. 3:8*). The soul constantly prefers Christ to all else, counting everything else that seeks to possess the heart but rubbish in comparison to him. Beloved peace; beloved human relationships; beloved wisdom and learning; beloved righteousness; beloved duties are all but rubbish compared to Christ.

The soul willingly accepts Christ as its only Husband, Lord and Saviour. This is called 'receiving' Christ (*John 1:12*). This does not mean a once-for-all act of the will, but a continual receiving of Christ in abiding with him and owning him to be our Lord for ever. This is when the soul agrees to take Christ on his terms, for Christ to save him as and how he

[59]

will and says, 'Lord, I would have had you and salvation in my own way and on my own terms, partly by my own efforts, by my own good works, but now I am willing to receive you and to be saved in your way, merely by grace. I would have walked according to the dictates of my own mind, yet now I give up myself to be wholly ruled by your Spirit, for in you alone I have righteousness and strength. In you alone I am justified, and in you alone do I glory.' In this way the soul has continual abiding communion with Christ in grace. This is what it means to receive Christ in his beauty and supreme glory. Let believers exercise their hearts abundantly in this communion. What joy they will find!

Let us, then, receive Christ in all his excellences and glories as he gives himself to us. Frequently think of him by faith, comparing him with other beloveds, such as sin, the world and legal righteousness. Then you will more and more prefer him above them all, and you will count them all as rubbish in comparison to him. And let your soul be persuaded of Christ's sincerity and willingness to give himself to you, in all that he is, to be yours for ever. And let us give up ourselves wholeheartedly to him. Let us tell Jesus that we will be for him and not for another. Let him hear this from us. He delights to hear it from our lips. Christ says, 'Your voice is sweet to my ears, and your face is beautiful in my eyes'. Are we going to disappoint Christ by neglecting this communion with him?

8: *The Glories and Excellences of Christ*

To encourage our hearts to give themselves up more fully to the Lord Jesus Christ, consider his glories and excellences.

CHRIST IS EXCEEDINGLY GLORIOUS AND EXCELLENT IN HIS DEITY

He is 'God blessed for evermore' (*Rom. 9:5*). He is 'the Lord our Righteousness' (*Jer. 23:6*). The angels in their highest glory hide their faces in his presence (*Isa. 6:2*).

Consider the endless, bottomless, boundless grace and compassion that is in Christ, the God of Zion. It is not the grace of a creature, nor all the grace that can possibly be found in any created nature, which will satisfy all our needs. We are too needy to be satisfied by a mere creature. But in Christ's human nature there is fulness of grace, for he did not receive 'the Spirit by measure' (*John 3:34*). In Christ there is a fulness like that of light in the sun, or of water in the sea. It is a fulness incomparably above the fulness of angels. Yet in Christ's human nature, it was a created and therefore a limited fulness. If Christ's human nature could be separated from his divine nature, then thirsty, guilty souls, would soon drain him dry. Christ's human nature on its own would not meet all our needs except in a moral way. But when the well of his humanity is inseparably united to the infinite, inexhaustible reservoir of his deity, who can possibly drain him dry?

The foundation of all peace, confidence and comfort lies in the grace and mercy of our Maker, the God of the whole earth. Kindness and power are also in him. He is our God and our kinsman Redeemer. He says to sinners, 'Look to me and be saved, for I am God and there is no other' (*Isa. 45:22*). And we can say, 'Surely in the Lord I have righteousness and strength' (*v. 24.*).

If all the world should drink free grace, mercy and pardon from Christ, the well of salvation; if they should draw strength from one single promise, they would not be able to lower the level of the water of grace in that promise one hair's breadth. There is enough grace, mercy and pardon in one of God's promises for the sins of millions of worlds, if they existed, because the promise is supplied from an infinite, bottomless reservoir. What is one finite guilt before this infinite and eternal reservoir of grace? Show me the sinner who can spread out his sins to infinite dimensions and I will show him this infinite and eternal reservoir of grace and mercy. Beware, then, of those who would rob you of the deity of Christ. If there were no more grace for me than what is treasured up in a mere creature, I would rejoice if my eternity was under rocks and mountains, hidden for ever from divine wrath.

Consider Christ's eternal, free, unchangeable love. If the love of Christ to us was the love of a mere man, though never so excellent, innocent and glorious, it must have a beginning and an end and could not possibly be infallibly effective. The love of Christ in his human nature to his people is more intense, kind, precious, compassionate, heightened as it was by an overwhelming sense of our sorrows, needs and temptations. Christ's love flows from that rich stock of grace, pity and compassion which was bestowed on him for our good and to supply us with all our needs. But yet this love of Christ's human nature alone cannot be infinite, nor eternal and nor can it be infallibly effective. Nor could he have said, 'As the Father has loved me, even so have I loved you' (*John 15:9*). His love, if merely human, could not be compared with and made equal to the divine love of the Father. Mere human love could not be eternally productive and unchangeable, which are the chief anchors of the soul that rests itself on the love of Christ.

Because Christ is God, his love is eternal. His love is eternal because he is eternal. Christ is 'the alpha and the omega, the first and the last, who is and who was and who is to come, the Almighty' (*Rev. 1:8, 11*).

Because Christ is God, his love is unchangeable. Our love is like ourselves. So the love of Christ is like himself. We love someone one day and hate him the next. But Jesus Christ is the same 'yesterday, today and forever' (*Heb. 13:8; 1:10–12*). Christ is the Lord and he does not change, therefore we are not consumed (*Mal. 3:6*). Christ's love had no beginning and will also have no end.

Because Christ is God, his love is infallibly effectual. A man may love another as his own soul, yet perhaps with all that love he can do nothing to help his friend. He may pity someone in prison, but be helpless to bring him any comfort. We may suffer with someone in trouble, and yet be unable to help. We cannot love grace into a child, nor mercy into a friend. We cannot love anyone into heaven, though we may greatly desire to do so. But the love of Christ, being the love of God, is infallibly effectual. It produces all the good things Christ desires to produce in his people. Christ loves life, grace and holiness into us. He loves us also into a covenant of love with himself. Christ loves us into heaven. Love in Christ is his will to do good to the one he loves. Whatever good Christ by his love wills to do to anyone is infallibly done to that person.

These three characteristics of Christ's love make his love exceedingly wonderful, and himself exceedingly desirable. How many millions of sins in every one of the elect, every sin sufficient to condemn them, has Christ's love overcome!

What mountains of unbelief has Christ's love removed! Look at the behaviour of any one saint. Consider his heart. See the many sinful stains and spots, the defilement and the weaknesses with which his life is contaminated, and tell me whether the love that bears with all this is not to be admired? And is not Christ's love the same to thousands every day? What streams of grace, purging, pardoning, quickening and helping, flow from Christ's love every day!

CHRIST IS EXCEEDINGLY EXCELLENT AND GREATLY TO BE DESIRED IN THE GLORY OF HIS HUMANITY

Christ's humanity is free from sin. He was the Lamb of God without spot and without blemish (*I Pet. 1:19*). He, as our high priest, 'is holy, harmless, undefiled and separate from sinners' (*Heb. 7:26*).

Objection. How could Christ take our nature and not the guilt and the defilements of it? If Levi paid tithes in Abraham, how is it that Christ did not sin in the loins of Adam? (*Heb. 7:9, 10*).

Answer. Christ was never legally represented by Adam, so was not liable to the imputation of Adam's sin. Had sin been imputed to Christ as a descendant of Adam, he would not have been a fit high priest to have offered sacrifices for us, for he would not have been 'separate from sinners' (*Heb. 7:26*). Had Adam not sinned, Christ would not have been incarnate. He would not have needed to be a Mediator for sinners. Therefore the moral necessity that Christ should be incarnate took place only after the fall. So Christ could not have been legally represented by Adam and so Adam's sin could not be imputed to him. Christ incarnate served God in a covenant of works in which he perfectly obeyed God without any sin. This he could not have done if Adam's sin had been imputed to him.

Neither did Christ inherit a polluted sinful nature from Adam. The substance of the virgin Mary from which Christ's human nature was made was sanctified by the Holy Spirit, so that the babe born was holy and undefiled (*Gal. 4:4; Luke 1:35*). From the moment of his conception in the womb of the virgin Mary, Christ was sanctified and set apart for that sacred work of saving sinners. By this sanctification of the Spirit, Christ is 'holy, harmless, undefiled and separate from sinners'. Peter tells us that he 'committed no sin, nor was guile found in his mouth' (*I Pet. 2:22*). He 'fulfilled all righteousness' (*Matt. 3:15*). His Father was always 'well pleased' with him because of his perfect obedience (*v. 17*). Such was Christ. Such is Christ. And yet for our sakes he was willing not only to be treated as the vilest of men, but also to undergo the punishment due to the vilest of sinners.

Christ's humanity is full of grace and so is both lovely and desirable. Christ was full of grace from the womb (*Luke 1:35*). He grew in the fulness of grace (*Luke 2:52*). All kinds of grace and all perfections of grace were in Christ and made up that fulness that was in him. But it is created grace that I intend to deal with.

Christ received the Holy Spirit, the reservoir of all grace, in full measure. And he received all the communications of grace from the Spirit, for 'it pleased the Father that in him all fulness should dwell' (*Col. 1:19*), so that in all things Christ should have the pre-eminence.

Christ is full of grace and truth. He is full and therefore sufficient to fulfil the purposes of grace. He was full of grace so as to be an example of obedience both to men and angels. He was full of grace so as to have uninterrupted communion with God. He is full of grace to supply all the needs of his people. He is full of grace to show forth the glory of the divine nature through his human nature. He is full of grace to bring his people to perfect victory over every trial and temptation.

He is full of grace to enable his people to obey every righteous and holy law of God. He is full of grace to the utmost capacity of a limited, created, finite nature. He is full of grace to bring the fullest pleasure and delight to his Father. He is full of grace as an everlasting monument to the glory of God in giving such inconceivable excellences to the Son of man.

This is the second thing to be considered to draw out our souls in love to our beloved Lord Jesus.

Consider that Christ is all this in one person. We have not been treating of two persons, a God and a man, but of one person who is both God and man. That which made the man Christ Jesus a man was the union of soul and body. And that which made him 'THE MAN', and without which he was not 'THE MAN', was the uniting of both natures, human and divine, in the person of the Son of God. From this union of the divine and the human natures in the person of the Son of God arise the grace, peace, life and security of the church.

Because Christ was God and man in one person, he was able to suffer and to bear whatever punishment was due to us. (Matt. 20:28; Acts 20:28; I John 3:16). There was room enough in Christ's breast to receive the points of all the swords that were sharpened by the law against us. And there was strength enough in Christ's shoulders to bear the burden of that curse that was due to us. It was because of this he was so willing to undertake the work of our redemption (*Heb. 10:7, 8*). If Christ had not been man, he could not have suffered for men, and if he had not been God, his suffering could not have satisfied infinite justice. If the great and righteous God had gathered together all the sins that had been committed by his chosen people from the foundation of the world, and searched the hearts of all that were to come to the end of the world, and then taken them all and laid them on a mere holy, innocent creature, they would have overwhelmed him and buried him for ever from the presence of God's love. So when the writer to the Hebrews talks of Christ purging our sin, he first describes his glorious powers (*Heb. 1:2, 3*). He and he alone was able to purge our sins.

Because Christ is both God and man in one person, he has become an endless, bottomless reservoir and source of grace to all those that believe. It pleased the Father to commit to Christ all the fulness of the Godhead. He is therefore the great treasury and storehouse of the church of God, not because of his manhood taken by itself, but as the God-man. So he is able to communicate grace to his people because he satisfied divine justice for their sins, merited all grace for them and purchased all grace for them. All grace first becomes his. All the things of the new covenant, the promises of God, all the mercy, love, grace and glory promised, first became his. They are all morally Christ's by covenant so that he may give them to his people as he thinks best.

The real communication of grace is by Christ sending the Holy Spirit to regenerate us and to create all habits of grace in us and to supply us daily with grace in our hearts. Now the Holy Spirit is sent by Christ as Mediator, and this he teaches his disciples (*John 14; 15; 16*). This is what I mean by this fulness of grace that is in Christ. This makes Christ the Alpha and Omega, the A and the Z of the church. He is the beginner and the finisher of our faith. Because of the great price Christ paid for our sins, and the full satisfaction he made to infinite justice, all grace became his to give to his people as he pleases. And Christ bestows grace on, or works it in, the hearts of his people by the Holy Spirit, as in his infinite wisdom he sees where it is most needed. How glorious Christ is to the soul when this is considered! All that we need is to be found in Christ. He is the life of our souls and the joy of our hearts because he is our Saviour from sin and our deliverer from the wrath to come.

Christ is the only one fit to be a Mediator between God and man

[67]

because he is both God and man in one person. So he is one with God and one with us and one in himself in the unity of his person. As Mediator, Christ is the 'power of God and the wisdom of God'. Through Christ the infinitely glorious wisdom of God shines out. What else do we need to know to encourage us to find our rest and peace in his bosom? Unbelief alone can hold us back from Christ. Nothing else is given to us to draw us to Christ other than this glorious revelation of him. This is the hidden mystery, great without controversy, the admiration and wonder of all believers to all eternity. Should not our thoughts and our hearts be always taken up with him?

Christ's excellence and glory lies also in this, that he is exalted and vested with all authority. When Jacob heard of the exaltation of his son Joseph in Egypt, and saw the chariots that he had sent for him, his spirit fainted within him and then revived, being filled with joy and longing desired to see his son again. We too may ask, Is our beloved Christ lost, who for our sakes lived in poverty on earth and who was persecuted, reviled and crucified? No! He was dead, but he is alive, and now he lives for ever and ever and has the keys of hell and death (*Rev. 1:18*). He is made a lord and ruler (*Acts 2:36*). God has set him as king on his holy hill of Zion (*Psa. 2:6*). All things are put in subjection under his feet (*Heb. 2:8*). He has been given 'all power in heaven and on earth' (*Matt. 28:18*). He has been given power 'over all flesh to give eternal life to those God had given him' (*John 17:2*). He rules his elect in the power of God (*Mic. 5:4*). He fills his enemies with fear, terror and horror until they yield him pretended obedience. Sometimes with outward judgments, Christ bruises, breaks and crushes them, staining his robes with their blood, filling the earth with their corpses. And at the last, Christ will gather them all together, the beast, the false prophet and all nations and will cast them into that lake that burns with fire and brimstone (*Psa. 110:6; Rev. 19:20*).

[68]

Christ is gloriously exalted above angels in this his authority, whether they be good or evil angels (*Eph. 1:20–22*). All are under his feet, at his command and his absolute right to deal with them as he pleases. Christ is at the right hand of God in the highest position possible. He is in full possession of a kingdom over the whole creation, having received a name that is above every name (*Phil. 2:9*). Christ is glorious on his throne, which is at the 'right hand of the majesty on high'. Christ is glorious in his name, a name above every name, that of 'Lord of lords and King of kings'. Christ is glorious in his sceptre: 'A sceptre of righteousness is the sceptre of his kingdom.' Christ is glorious in his attendants. 'His chariots are twenty thousand, even thousands of angels.' Among them he rides on the heavens and sends out the voice of his strength, attended with ten thousand, even thousands of his holy ones. Christ is glorious in his subjects. All creatures in heaven and on earth are put in subjection to him. Nothing is left that is not put in subjection to him. Christ is glorious in the way he rules, and how he administers his kingdom. He rules with sweet effectiveness and with serene power. He rules in righteousness, holiness and grace in and to his elect. He rules with terror, vengeance and certain destruction towards the rebellious angels and men. Christ is glorious in the outcome of his kingdom when every knee shall bow before him, and all shall stand before his judgment seat. And after all this, what a small part of his glory have we pointed to! This is the Christ with whom we have communion and fellowship.

CHRIST IN THE SONG OF SONGS, CHAPTER 5

We shall now see how the Shulamite describes her beloved, and see how wonderful a description this is of Christ (*Song 5:10–16*). We have already considered verse 10.

The Shulamite begins by describing his head and face (*vv. 11–13*).

His head is like the finest gold (Song 5:11)

Two things are chiefly to be noted in gold: its splendour or glory and its durability. Christ's head is his government, authority and kingdom (*Psa. 21:3*). So Christ's head is here said to be gold, because of the crown of gold that adorns it. In Nebuchadnezzar's dream he saw an image whose head was of gold (*Dan. 2:38*). This symbolised the monarchy that was most eminent for glory. And these two characteristics, splendour and durability, are chiefly to be seen in the kingdom and authority of Christ.

Christ's kingdom is a glorious kingdom. Christ is full of glory and majesty and in his majesty he rides 'prosperously' (*Psa. 45:3, 4; 21:5, 6*). Christ's kingdom is a heavenly, spiritual, universal and unshaken kingdom. All these make his kingdom a glorious kingdom.

Christ's kingdom is a durable kingdom, a kingdom of solid gold (*Psa. 45:6; Isa. 11:7; Dan. 7:27; 2:44*). Christ 'must reign until he has put all enemies under his feet' (*I Cor. 15:25*). This is that head of gold, the splendour and eternity of his government.

And if you take the head in its natural sense, either the glory of his deity is here meant, or the fulness and excellence of his wisdom. The allegory is not to be too narrowly defined if we keep to the analogy of faith.

His locks are wavy, and black as a raven (Song 5:11)

Interpreting this in a political sense, his locks symbolise his thoughts, counsels and ways in the administration of his kingdom. His locks are black or dark because of the depth and unsearchableness of his thoughts, as God is said to dwell in thick darkness. His locks are wavy, falling in perfect order and beauty, symbolising the order and beauty of his infinite wisdom. His thoughts are as many as the hairs of the head, seemingly entangled and confused, but really falling in perfect order and beauty, deep and unsearchable, dreadful to his enemies, but full of beauty to his beloved people. Such are the thoughts of his heart and the counsels of his wisdom in the administration of his kingdom. They are dark, puzzling and confused to the unbeliever, but to Christ's saints his thoughts are deep, many and ordered in all things, full of beauty and utterly desirable.

In a natural sense, black and wavy locks denote beauty and youthful strength. The strength and power of Christ, as he works out his counsels in all his ways, appears glorious and lovely.

His eyes are like doves by the rivers of waters, washed with milk, and fitly set (Song 5:12)

Doves are gentle birds. They are not birds of prey. Of all birds, doves have the brightest, shiniest and most piercing of eyes. Their delight also in streams of water is well known. Their being washed in milk, or clear, white crystal water, adds to their beauty. So his eyes are like doves.

His eyes are also fitly set. They are in perfect positions for beauty and brightness, as a precious stone is set in a ring, as the word signifies. Eyes symbolise the knowledge, the understanding and the discerning spirit of Christ Jesus. In this description, the eyes of the beloved illustrate kindness, purity, discernment and glory.

Christ's kindness and compassion to his church is signified. Christ looks on his church with doves' eyes, that is, with kindness and compassion. Towards his church he has no anger or thoughts of vengeance. As God's eyes were on the land of Canaan, and as he cared for that land, so his eyes are on the church, on each one of his people as one that in kindness and compassion cares for us and uses his wisdom, knowledge and understanding on our behalf (*Deut. 11:12*). Christ is the stone, that foundation stone of the church, on which are 'seven eyes' (*Zech. 3:9*). In Christ there is perfect wisdom, knowledge, care and kindness for the church's guidance.

The purity of Christ's eyes is signified. Christ 'is of purer eyes than to behold evil, and cannot look on wickedness' (*Hab. 1:13*). Christ is 'not a God who takes pleasure in wickedness, nor shall evil dwell with him. The boastful shall not stand in his sight' (*Psa. 5:4, 5*). If righteous Lot was disturbed when he saw the filthy deeds of wicked men, and he only had impure eyes, how much more do the purer eyes of our dear Lord Jesus loathe all the filthiness of sinners. It shows how much he loves us, that he is concerned to take away our filth and stains, so that his pure eyes may rest on us with pleasure and delight. We are so defiled that we could do nothing to make ourselves pure and clean. So Christ cleansed us by his own blood. He undertook to present to himself a glorious church, holy and without blemish (*Eph. 5:25–27*). His eyes are so pure that he could not look at the church with joy and delight in any other condition. Christ is not satisfied with his spouse, the church, until he can say of her, 'You are all fair, my love, and there is no spot in you' (*Song 4:7*). Christ takes away our spots and stains by the 'renewing of the Holy Spirit'. He covers us completely with his own righteousness. This he does because his eyes are so pure that 'they cannot look on evil.' His purpose is to present us to himself a holy people.

Christ's discernment is signified. Christ sees as doves see. He sees quickly, clearly, thoroughly. He sees through to the bottom of that which he looks at. His eyes are described as 'a flame of fire' (*Rev. 1:14*). They are described as 'flames of fire', so that the churches might know that he is the one who 'searches the minds and hearts' (*Rev. 2:23*). Whilst he was in the world, it was said of him that he 'knew all men, and had no need that anyone should testify of man, for he knew what was in man' (*John 2:24, 25*). Christ's piercing eyes look through all the thick coverings of hypocrites and the show they put on to deceive. Christ sees what men are in reality, what they are thinking in their hearts, for 'as a man thinks in his heart, so is he'. He does not see as we see. He considers and takes note of the hidden man of the heart. No humble, broken, contrite soul shall lose one sigh or groan that arises from a desire to find him and have communion with him. Christ sees in secret. No glorious performance of the most glorious hypocrite will be of any use. Christ's eyes see through all, and the filth of the hypocrites' hearts lies naked and exposed before him.

Christ's beauty and glory are also meant. Everything about Christ is beautiful, for he is 'altogether lovely' (*Song 5:16*). He is the wisdom of God's eternal wisdom. His understanding is infinite. What spots and stains are in all our knowledge. Even when our knowledge is made perfect, it will still be finite and limited. But Christ is without one spot of darkness and without the tiniest speck of limitation. So Christ is beautiful and glorious.

His cheeks are like a bed of spices, like banks of scented herbs (*Song 5:13*)

The cheeks of a man show beauty and courage. The beauty of Christ is from his fulness of grace. His courage is revealed in his rule and government arising from that universal authority that has been given to him. This beauty and courage the church calls his cheeks. So the church describes Christ as spiritually beautiful and desirable.

The saints smell a sweet perfume of grace in Christ (*Song 1:3*). It is this grace in which they rest, in which they delight, and from which they are spiritually refreshed and strengthened. As the scent of flowers pleases the natural sense of smell, refreshes the spirits, and delights the person, so the graces of Christ please, refresh and delight the saints.

Order and beauty are symbolised by the 'banks of scented herbs'. When herbs are set out in order, anyone may know what herb he needs at that time. This is so with the graces of Christ. In the gospel, the graces of Christ are distinctly set out in order so that sinners by faith may see them and take what they need. The graces of Christ are set in order for the saints in the promises of the gospel. The believer sees all the graces of Christ and takes by faith and prayer what he needs for that moment. One takes light and joy, and another life and power. So the covenant is said to be 'ordered in all things' (*II Sam. 23:5*).

The graces of Christ are also seen to be outstanding and remarkable as the beloved's cheeks are outstanding and remarkable. The graces of Christ are held out and lifted up by the preaching of the gospel so that they might be clearly seen by all.

His lips are lilies, dripping liquid myrrh (Song 5:13)

The glory of colour is seen in the lilies, and sweet perfume is smelled in the myrrh. The glory and beauty of the lilies is compared by Christ to 'Solomon in all his glory' (*Matt. 6:29*). It is said of Christ that grace is poured on his lips (*Psa. 45:2*). So men wondered and were amazed at the words of grace that came from his mouth. So Christ's lips dripped sweet-smelling myrrh. In this Christ is excellent and glorious indeed. So those that preach his word to the saving of souls are said to be 'the fragrance of Christ' to God (*II Cor. 2:15*). The fragrance of the knowledge of God is diffused through them (*II Cor. 2:14*). What the Holy Spirit means to show us is that the word of Christ is sweet, fragrant and precious to believers. Believers see Christ to be excellent, desirable and beautiful in his commands, promises, exhortations and even in the most bitter warnings.

His hands are rods of gold set with beryl (Song 5:14)

Rods or rings of gold set with precious stones are both valuable and desirable, both for profit and for ornament. So are the hands of Christ, which symbolise all his works. All Christ's works are glorious. They are all fruits of his wisdom, love and generosity.

His body is carved ivory inlaid with sapphires (Song 5:14)

The smoothness and brightness of ivory, the preciousness and heavenly colour of sapphires are here used to describe the glory and beauty of Christ. To these, his body – or rather his heart – is compared. They describe the glory of Christ's feelings and emotions, the tender and unspeakable love and kindness to his church and people. What a beautiful sight it is to the eye to see pure, polished ivory inlaid with heaps of precious sapphires. But how much more glorious are the tender feelings, mercies and compassion of the Lord Jesus to believers.

His legs are pillars of marble set on bases of fine gold. His countenance is like Lebanon, excellent as the cedars. His mouth is most sweet (Song 5:15, 16)

These words symbolise the strength of Christ's kingdom, the faithfulness and stability of his promises, the height and glory of his person and dominion, and the sacredness and wonder of communion with him.

Yes, Christ is altogether lovely (Song 5:15)

He is altogether lovely in his person, in the glorious all-sufficiency of his deity and the gracious purity and holiness of his humanity, authority, majesty, love and power.

He is altogether lovely in his birth and incarnation.

He is altogether lovely in the whole of his life, in his holiness and obedience, which in the depths of poverty and persecution he showed by doing good, receiving evil, blessing others and being cursed himself all his days.

He is altogether lovely in his death, especially to sinners. He was never more glorious and desirable than when he was taken down from the cross, broken and lifeless. He carried all our sins into a land of forgetfulness. He made peace and reconciliation for us. He procured life and immortality for us.

He is altogether lovely in his work, in his great undertaking to be the Mediator between God and man, to glorify God's justice, to save our souls, to bring us to the enjoyment of God who were at such an infinite distance from him by reason of our sin.

He is altogether lovely in the glory and majesty with which he was crowned. Now he is seated at the right hand of the majesty on high. Though he is terrible to his enemies, yet he is full of mercy, love and compassion to his loved ones.

He is altogether lovely in all those graces and comforts that he pours on his people by the Holy Spirit.

He is altogether lovely in all the tender care, power and wisdom by which he protects, safeguards and delivers his church and people in the midst of all oppositions and persecutions to which they are exposed.

He is altogether lovely in all his ordinances and the whole of that glorious spiritual worship which he has appointed for his people, by which they draw near to him and have communion with him and his Father.

He is altogether lovely and glorious in the vengeance that he takes and will finally execute upon the stubborn enemies of himself and his people.

He is altogether lovely in the pardon that he has purchased and which he gives to those who receive him.

He is altogether lovely in the reconciliation that he has wrought, in the grace that he communicates, in the comforts, the peace and the joy that he gives his saints, and in his assured preservation of them, losing none but raising all of them to eternal glory in the last day.

'Yes, he is altogether lovely. This is my beloved, and this is my friend, O daughters of Jerusalem' (*Song. 5:16*).

9: *The Wisdom and Knowledge of Christ*

The second excellent characteristics of Christ, the Son of God, that will endear our hearts to him and persuade us to receive him are his wisdom and knowledge. All true and solid knowledge is laid up in Christ, so if we would be truly wise and come to true knowledge, we must come to it by Christ.

Right from the beginning, man sought to be wise. But he sought wisdom independently of God. The Christian has learned that all true wisdom is laid up in Christ and that it is to be obtained from him alone.

The Holy Spirit tells us that 'Christ is the power of God and the wisdom of God' (*I Cor. 1:24*). By this is not meant the essential wisdom of God as he is the eternal Son of the Father, but that wisdom of God displayed in him as crucified (*I Cor. 1:23*). Christ crucified is the wisdom of God in the salvation of sinners. It is this wisdom that makes foolish all the wisdom of the world, all the world's ideas of how sinners can be saved. Salvation for sinners is held out in Christ, by Christ and to be had only from Christ. So in Christ crucified we see the glory of God (*II Cor. 3:18*). Not only is Christ said to be 'the wisdom of God', but also to be 'made to us wisdom' (*I Cor. 1:30*). Christ is made wisdom to us, not by creation, but by ordination and appointment. He not only teaches us wisdom as the great prophet of the church, but also because by knowing him we become acquainted with the wisdom of God. Christ, then, is our wisdom for 'in him are hidden all the treasures of wisdom and knowledge' (*Col. 2:3*).

There are two sorts of wisdom in the world. There is civil wisdom and prudence for the managing of daily affairs, and there is the ability to learn and produce art and literature. But

God rejects both these as of no use at all in the work which true wisdom intends to accomplish (*I Cor. 1:19, 20*). There is no true wisdom or knowledge apart from the knowledge of God (*Jer. 8:9*). True wisdom and knowledge are shut up in Jesus Christ. He alone is 'the true light which gives light to every man who comes into the world' (*John 1:9*). He who does not come to Christ walks in darkness.

God, by his work of creation, revealed his power, goodness, wisdom and all-sufficiency to his creatures who are capable of knowing (*Rom. 1:19–21*). But the work of creation cannot in any way reveal his patience, longsuffering and forbearance, which are other properties of his nature (*Exod. 34:6, 7*).

So God, by the works of providence in preserving and ruling the world, reveals his patience, longsuffering and forbearance. By cursing the earth and filling it with signs of his anger and indignation against men's sins, he has 'revealed from heaven his wrath against all ungodliness and unrighteousness of men' (*Rom. 1:18*). And by not destroying all things at once, he reveals his patience and forbearance to all (*Acts 14:16, 17*). The psalmist also describes his goodness and wisdom (*Psa. 104*). Paul tells us that God 'endured with much longsuffering the vessels of wrath prepared for destruction' (*Rom. 9:22*). But the chief and most glorious properties of God's nature are revealed only in and by Jesus Christ.

God's love to sinners is gloriously revealed in and by Jesus Christ. Without his love, man is of all creatures the most miserable and he will not have the least glimpse of this love except in Christ. The Holy Spirit says, 'God is love' (*I John 4:8, 16*). By this is meant not only that God has a loving nature, but also that he purposed to love sinners with an eternal love, and this love is revealed through Jesus Christ (*I John 4:9*). The wisdom of the world is foolishness because that wisdom which cannot teach me that 'God is love' is foolishness.

But to know that 'God is love' would be fruitless if we did not also know his pardoning mercy or grace. Adam did not know this pardoning mercy, nor did he have any hope of it, for when he sinned, he ran and hid from God (*Gen. 3:18*). Pardoning mercy comes by Christ alone. This pardoning mercy is revealed in the gospel, and in this pardoning mercy God will be glorified for ever (*Eph. 1:6*). Pardoning mercy is not a vague general mercy which overlooks sin. This would be dishonouring to God. Pardoning mercy is God's free, gracious acceptance of a sinner because satisfaction was made to his justice consistent with his glory. It is a mercy of inconceivable wonder, for God came down from the heights of glory to bring forgiveness to sinners, whilst at the same time exacting justice and severity on sin. His righteousness is also revealed in the forgiveness of sin (*Rom. 3:25*). Therefore it is everywhere said that forgiveness of sins is wholly to be found in Christ (*Eph. 1:7*). So this gospel grace and pardoning mercy are purchased by Christ alone and revealed in Christ alone.

The main purpose of all the Old Testament institutions was to show the truth that remission and forgiveness is wholly wrapped up in the Lord Christ, and that out of Christ nothing at all can be known of God's pardoning mercy and nor can the least morsel of it be tasted apart from Christ. If God had not set forth the Lord Christ, all the angels in heaven and men on earth could not have known that there had been any such pardoning mercy in the nature of God. Paul teaches that in Christ the full revelation as well as the exercise of this mercy is to be seen in Christ alone, both in his being sent and his being declared and preached in the gospel. So this pardoning mercy and salvation was not discovered by 'good works'.

Love to sinners and pardoning mercy are the properties of God by which he will be known, and whoever does not know God as the God who loves and shows pardoning mercy to sinners does not know him at all. They know an idol and not the only true God. John tells us that 'whoever denies the Son does not have the Father either; he who acknowledges the Son has the Father also' (*I John 2:23*). And not to have God as Father is not to have him at all. God is known as a Father only as he is love and full of pardoning mercy in Christ. How this knowledge is to be had the Holy Spirit tells us (*I John 5:20*). By Christ alone we have that understanding which enables us to know him that is true. These properties of God, Christ reveals in his doctrines and in the revelation he makes of God and his will. This he does as the great prophet of the church (*John 17:6*). But the life which comes from this knowledge lies in personally knowing Christ, because he is 'the brightness of the Father's glory and the express image of his person' (*Heb. 1:3*).

There are other properties of God which, though revealed by other means, yet are clearly, supremely and savingly revealed only in Christ.

God's justice in punishing sin is supremely revealed in Christ. God has in many ways shown his indignation and wrath against sin so that men cannot but know that it is 'the judgment of God that they who commit such things are worthy of death' (*Rom. 1:32*). In many providential happenings 'the wrath of God is revealed from heaven against all ungodliness of men' (*Rom. 1:18*). So men must say that he is a God of judgment.

God's justice cast the angels who sinned out of heaven, shutting them up under chains of everlasting darkness to the judgment of the great day.

God's justice also condemned and overthrew Sodom and Gomorrah so that they might be examples of his judgment on the ungodly (*II Pet. 2:6*).

But God's justice shines most brightly in the Lord Christ.

[81]

In Christ, God has shown his righteousness. He showed that it was impossible for his justice to be turned away from sinners without propitiation, a victim who would suffer in the place of sinners, so satisfying divine justice and so turning away God's wrath on sinners. God did not spare his only Son, but made his soul an offering for sin, and would be satisfied with no atonement but that which he purchased by his blood. It has been abundantly shown that God's righteousness and holiness required such an atonement to show God's wrath against sin and his determination to punish sin. To know that it was necessary for God's justice to be carried out on sin is the only true and useful knowledge of God's justice. To think that God can exercise justice as he pleases does not make justice a property of his nature, but a free act of his will. To condemn and punish where justice does not condemn nor require punishment is not justice, but an act of ill-will.

In the penalty inflicted on Christ for sin, God's justice is far more gloriously revealed than in any other way. To see a world made good and beautiful, wrapped up in wrath and curses, clothed with thorns and briers, made subject to vanity and in bondage to corruption; to hear it groan in pain under that burden; to consider legions of angels, the most glorious and immortal of creatures, cast down to hell, bound with chains of darkness and kept for a more dreadful judgment, and that for one sin; to see the oceans of blood spilt on account of sin will give some insight into God's justice and righteousness. But what is all this to that which we see with the spiritual eye in the Lord Christ? All these examples of God's justice are but worms and of no value compared to God's justice seen in Christ.

To see Christ, the wisdom and the power of God, always beloved of the Father, fear and tremble, bow and sweat, pray and die; to see him lifted up on the cross, the earth trembling beneath him as if unable to bear his weight; to see the heavens darkened over him as if shut against his cry and himself hanging between both as if refused by each; and to see that all this is because of our sins is to see clearly the holy justice and wrath of God against sin. Supremely in Christ do we learn this great truth that God hates sin and judges it with a dreadful and fearful judgment.

God's patience, forbearance and longsuffering towards sinners is supremely revealed and seen in Christ. There are many glimpses of the patience of God shining out in the work of his providence. But all these are but nothing compared to the patience, forbearance and longsuffering towards sinners shown in Christ.

In Christ, the patience, forbearance and longsuffering of God towards sinners is seen in that he does not immediately punish men for their sins. It is seen in God's continual goodness to wicked men, causing his sun to shine upon them and sending rain and fruitful seasons, filling their hearts with food and gladness. But all this is but darkness compared to the light shone on God's patience, forbearance and longsuffering to sinners in Christ. This revelation in Christ is entirely of another kind. In Christ the very nature of God is seen to be one of love and kindness and that he wills to show this love and kindness to sinners. In Christ, God has promised, sworn and solemnly committed himself by covenant to show this love and kindness to sinners. And to make sure that we do not worry about whether God will show love and kindness to us, we have a sure and stable foundation on which to rest and assure ourselves, namely the reconciliation and atonement that is made in the blood of Christ. But there would be little comfort for us if it was not revealed that the other properties of God, namely his justice and wrath against sin, had been fully satisfied by Christ. So God is said to be 'in Christ reconciling the world to himself' (*II Cor. 5:19*).

In Christ, the patience, forbearance and longsuffering of God towards sinners is full of love, sweetness, kindness and grace. A sinner out of Christ thinks that because God does not at once punish sin, God will never call him to account. So he perishes full of faith in God's forbearance. But in Christ, God is revealed as waiting to be gracious to sinners; waiting to show them love and kindness (*Isa. 30:18*). When the soul sees and is convinced that God, for Christ's sake, has overlooked his many sins, he is astonished that God should do this. He is amazed that God did not cast him out of his sight. Instead, the redeemed soul finds that with infinite wisdom God has delivered his soul from the power of the devil, dealt with his sins and brought his soul into fellowship with himself. God has made a way for the complete forgiveness of our sins through his forbearance, and this way is to be found only in Christ.

In Christ, the patience, forbearance and longsuffering of God leaves unrepentant and unbelieving sinners without excuse, so that his power and wrath against sin might be shown in their just and righteous destruction (*Rom. 9:22*). Therefore God allowed 'them to walk in their own ways', which is shown to be a most dreadful judgment (*Acts 14:16; Psa. 81:12*). To be given up to our own heart's lusts and to be left to walk according to our own ideas is as dreadful a condition as a creature is capable of falling into in this world.

In contrast, God's purpose to show patience, forbearance and longsuffering to sinners in Christ is to save those whom he has chosen to save and to bring them by Christ to himself. Therefore Peter tells Christians that God is 'longsuffering towards us, not willing that any should perish but that all should come to repentance' (*II Pet. 3:9*). That is, all to whom God shows longsuffering and forbearance, for that is the purpose of this statement, so that his will concerning our repentance and salvation may be accomplished. God's purpose in his infinite wisdom and goodness is that we should not be destroyed in spite of our sins (*Isa. 54:9*). So Paul describes God as the 'God of patience and comfort' (*Rom. 15:5*). God's patience is a matter of the greatest comfort. The treasures, then, of God's patience, forbearance and longsuffering bringing great comfort to sinners are stored up in Christ, and none can experience these properties of God except by Christ.

In Christ, we see God's infinite wisdom in working all things for His own glory and the good of those whom he has chosen to love. The Lord has indeed shown clearly his infinite wisdom in his works of creation, providence and the government of his world. In wisdom he has made all his creatures (*Psa. 104:24*). God's infinite wisdom is also seen in his providence, his upholding all things and guiding them so that they will fulfil the purpose of their existence to his own glory. In these things we learn that God is 'wonderful in counsel and excellent in guidance' (*Isa. 28:29*). God's law is also to be admired as an expression of his wisdom (*Deut. 4:7, 8*).

But in contrast, it is only in Christ that we plumb 'the depths of the riches of the wisdom and knowledge of God' (*Rom. 11:33*). So Christ is said to be 'the wisdom of God' and to be 'made to us wisdom'. Christ is that 'mystery, that hidden wisdom, which God ordained before the world was, which none of the princes of this world knew' (*I Cor. 2:7, 8*). He is that 'manifold wisdom of God' (*Eph. 3:10*). God, in the beginning, made all things good, glorious and beautiful and showed clearly his wisdom and goodness. Now all that beauty has been defaced by sin, and the whole creation rolled up in darkness, wrath, curses and confusion, burying the great praises of God under it. Man, especially, was utterly lost and came short of that glory of God for which he was created (*Rom. 3:23*). Now, in the face of all this, the depth of the riches of the wisdom and knowledge of God is seen most gloriously in Christ. God's purpose in Christ shines out from his heart, a purpose that was hidden there from eternity. This purpose was to restore all things to a state infinitely above that which was first created to the praise of his glorious wisdom and goodness. God's purpose also was to raise sinners to an inconceivably better condition than they were in before sin entered the world. God now appears more glorious than ever he did before. Now he is seen to be a God who pardons iniquity and sin and who is infinitely rich in grace (*Eph. 1:6*). God also has infinitely vindicated his justice in the sight of men, angels and devils in setting forth his Son for a propitiation. We are also more firmly established in God's favour and are being carried forward to a much greater weight of glory than was revealed before. It is no wonder, then, that Paul exclaims, 'great is the mystery of godliness' (*I Tim. 3:16*). We receive 'grace for grace'. That grace lost in Adam is replaced by that infinitely better grace in Christ. This is deep wisdom indeed. The love of Christ to his church and his union with his church Paul declares to be 'a great mystery' (*Eph. 5:32*).

All this is hidden in Christ. The great and unspeakable riches of God's wisdom in pardoning sin, saving sinners, satisfying justice, fulfilling the law, regaining his own honour and providing for us a much greater weight of glory are all accomplished in Christ. And all this was accomplished out of an impossible state of affairs. It was impossible for angels or men to discover how God could possibly restore all things to his glory or ever save one sinful creature from everlasting ruin. So it is said that, at the last day, God 'shall be glorified in his saints, and admired in all those who believe.' (*II Thess. 1:10*). To save sinners through believing will be seen to be a far more wonderful work than to create the world out of nothing.

[86]

In Christ, God's all-sufficiency is wonderfully revealed. God's all-sufficiency is his absolute and universal perfection by which there is nothing lacking in him, and nor is he in need of anything outside of himself. Nothing can be added to his fulness and nor can he ever be emptied of his fulness. There is also in God an all-sufficiency for others also. From his all-sufficiency, God has power to impart and communicate his goodness and himself so as to satisfy and fill his creatures to their utmost capacity with whatever is good for them and with whatever they desire. God showed his all-sufficiency abundantly in creation. He made all things good, all things perfect. In other words, his creation lacked nothing, each in its own kind. In this way, God stamped his goodness on all creation. And God's giving of himself as an all-sufficient God, to be enjoyed by his creatures, to provide for all their needs out of himself, is only revealed in Christ. In Christ, God is in covenant with his people to be a Father to them. And in this covenant he has promised to lay out himself as the one who alone can meet the needs of his creatures. In Christ, God has promised to give himself to them for their eternal good and to be their exceedingly great reward.

Nothing in God concerning our salvation can be known or received except by Christ. All that is necessary for our salvation is in Christ and is shown to us by Christ. All truth outside Christ does not lead to the knowledge of salvation. It only leads to further corruption (*Rom. 2:4, 5; 1:18–23*).

In order that we may know God's purpose and way of salvation and come to enjoy its comforts, we must be convinced of three things.

(1) We must be convinced that his justice, righteousness, patience, goodness, mercy, forbearance and all his works of creation and providence are all glorified in doing us good and not evil. It will be no comfort to us to know that God is

infinitely righteous, just and holy, unchangeably true and faithful, if we believe that he will glorify these properties in our ruin and destruction. Of what comfort will it be to us to know that God is patient and forbearing if I am one of those vessels fitted for destruction? Of what use will it be to hear him proclaim, 'The Lord, the Lord, merciful and gracious, abundant in goodness and truth' if I am one of those guilty ones whom he will not clear? Outside Christ, then, knowledge of God's justice will only make sinners want to run away and hide (*Gen. 3; Isa. 2:21; 33:15, 16*). To know that God is patient will only increase our stubbornness (*Eccles. 8:11*). To know that God is holy will only deter us from coming to him (*John 24:19*).

But in Christ, all these glorious properties of God fill us with joy and comfort, for in him we are convinced that they are all glorified in our salvation and God's goodness to us. In Christ, God glorified his justice by punishing his Son for our sins (*Rom. 3:25; 8:33, 34*). In Christ, God has glorified his truth and faithfulness in fulfilling his threatenings and promises. God's curse on sinners was borne by Christ (*Gal. 3:13*). And in Christ, all the promises of God are fulfilled (*II Cor. 1:20*). And how gloriously in Christ are God's mercy, goodness and the riches of his grace seen to be!

This is true saving knowledge to know that, in Christ, God is glorified and exalted in doing us good. But this wisdom is hidden only in Jesus Christ.

(2) We must be convinced that God will use all his glorious properties for our good. How do we know that God will save us when we see so many perishing everlastingly? Only in Christ can we know that God will use all his properties for our salvation. He has set forth Christ to be 'the Lord our righteousness' (*Isa. 45:24, 25*). God has made Christ to us, 'wisdom, righteousness, sanctification and redemption'. He is the captain of salvation to those that believe. So God is said

to be 'in Christ, reconciling the world to himself' (*II Cor. 5:18*).

(3) We must be convinced that these attributes of God are powerful and able to bring us into eternal glory. To assure us of this, the Lord wraps up the whole covenant of grace in one promise: 'I will be your God.' In being our God, all his attributes work for us and our eternal good. To convince us further still, he says, 'I am God Almighty. I am wholly able to perform all I have promised. I will also be your exceedingly great reward. I am the all-sufficient God.' Now we know that this covenant is confirmed by the blood of Christ. Only in Christ is God all-sufficient and our exceedingly great reward. So Christ is said 'to save to the uttermost those that come to God by him'.

Only in Christ, then, can we be assured that God intends to do us good, will do us good and is able to do us good. Only in Christ can God save us and bring us into eternal glory and blessedness.

To know Christ and to be in Christ by faith is to know the wonder and excellence of the wisdom and knowledge of God in the salvation of sinners.

If we wish to have fellowship with the Son of God, then it is part of our wisdom to know ourselves. The Holy Spirit was sent to convince the world 'of sin, of righteousness and of judgment' (*John 16:8*). To know ourselves in respect of sin, righteousness and judgment is true and sound wisdom.

Knowing ourselves in respect of sin. There is an awareness and knowledge of sin left naturally in the consciences of men (*Rom. 2:14, 15*). So man knows 'the judgment of God, that they who do such things are worthy of death' (*Rom. 1:32*). All men in every nation have some sense of sin and of God's hatred of sin. The very first idea men have of God in this world is that he is a rewarder of good and evil. From this knowledge rose all the sacrifices, purgings and expiations man has invented to placate an angry God.

A further knowledge of sin came by the law. 'By the law is the knowledge of sin' (*Rom. 3:20*). And 'the law was added because of transgressions' (*Gal. 3:19*).

The law in all its purity, holiness and perfection reveals the pollution of sin. The way the law was given revealed God's wrath on sin and filled man with dread and terror as he heard the thunder and felt the earthquakes.

When man sees sin bringing death, and when he lies under God's curse and wrath, then he begins to understand the great sinfulness of sin. Yet man still does not have a true and thorough conviction of sin, and will not have it until Christ sends his Spirit to convince him of sin (*John 16:8*). So only by Christ is to be found the true knowledge of sin, firstly by his being made sin for us, and secondly by his work of saving us from our sins.

Consider what sin deserved. It was his only Son that God sent into the world to suffer for sin (*John 3:16; Rom. 8:32*). Never was sin seen to be more abominably sinful than when the punishment of it fell upon the Son of God. When God made his Son to be sin for us, he showed how utterly impossible it was for him to let the least sin go unpunished.

God was not pleased with the blood, the tears, the cries and the terrible torments of the Son of his love. But God required that his law be fulfilled, his justice satisfied and his wrath propitiated for sin. Nothing less than the death of his Son could fulfil these requirements. So if we would learn the real truth about sin, we must look at Christ crucified.

Consider what Christ suffered. It pleased God to bruise him, to put him to grief, to make his soul an offering for sin and to pour out his life even to death. God hid himself from his Son and caused him to cry out, 'My God, my God, why have you forsaken me?' God made him to be sin and a curse for us. Such was Christ's suffering. He sweated great drops of blood, was grievously troubled and his soul was deeply distressed even to death. He that was the power and wisdom of God stooped under the burden of sin until the whole of nature was amazed and hid itself in darkness. All this shows God's hatred and loathing of sin. Sin brought the Son of God from the heights of heaven to the depths of hell.

Consider man's weakness and utter inability to save himself from his sins. This is the second thing to be learned from the cross.

Man is utterly unable to make any atonement with God for sin. The prophet Micah shows man's helplessness in the face of God to find any atonement for sin (*Mic. 6:6, 7*). David also shows that no-one 'can by any means redeem his brother, nor give to God a ransom for him; for the redemption of their souls is costly' (*Psa. 49:7, 8*).

God has said that no sacrifices, even those he appointed,

could atone for sin (*Heb. 10:11; 9.9*). Rejecting these sacrifices, Christ in their stead says, 'Behold, I have come, to do your will, O God' (*Heb. 10:6–8*). So it is by Christ that we are 'justified from all things from which we could not be justified by the law' (*Acts 13:39*).

God has also written foolishness on all other attempts to atone for sin, by setting forth his Son 'to be a propitiation' (*Rom. 3:24–26*). For 'if righteousness were by the law, then Christ died in vain' (*Gal. 2:21*). It was when we were weak and without strength that God sent his Son (*Rom. 5:6, 8, 9*).

Man is utterly unable to obey God and to live in agreement with God. This is one truth that man finds the greatest difficulty in learning. He rises up in pride and anger at this truth, denying it with all his being. From where, then, can man learn this truth? Nature does not teach it. The law does not teach it. This truth lies hidden in the Lord Jesus (*Rom. 8:2–4*). The law can never bring man to a perfect righteousness, for man can never perfectly obey the law. Man's fleshly nature, being corrupted by sin, has been made weak and unable to obey the law.

Only Christ can bring man to a perfect righteousness. Christ does this by paying the punishment for our sin and setting us free from its guilt, and by imputing to us his perfect righteousness and so setting us free from having to justify ourselves by our own attempted self-righteousness. Secondly, Christ enables us to obey the law by his Spirit working in us and imparting to us his righteousness. Only this truth convinces us of our utter inability to obey God by our own strength and ability.

Consider the utter inability of man to root out and to destroy the power of sin in his life. The power of sin in our mortal bodies may be hindered because the body has been in some way or other disabled and so cannot serve the lusts of the flesh. But the power of sin is still there. Sin is never more alive than when it is unable to serve its lusts.

But it is only in Christ that the root and power of sin can be destroyed (*Rom. 6:3–6*). Christ was crucified for us, therefore sin was crucified in us. Christ died for us and so the body of sin was destroyed so that we should no longer serve sin. And as Christ was raised from the dead so that death shall have no more dominion over him, so also we are raised from sin that it should have no more dominion over us. This wisdom is hidden in Christ alone.

Moses on his dying day had all his strength and vigour. So has sin and the law to all who are not in Christ. At its dying day, sin has in no way lost any of its strength and vigour. So to be truly acquainted with the principle of dying to sin, to feel strength and power flowing from the cross of Christ overcoming sin in us, to find sin crucified in us as Christ was crucified for us is wisdom indeed.

The whole purpose of sin and why God allowed sin into the world is revealed only in Christ. Sin was allowed entry into the world in order that God's glorious grace may be praised in the pardoning and forgiveness of sin. Outside Christ, sin in its own nature only brings dishonour to God. But in Christ, God is seen to be a God pardoning iniquity, transgression and sin.

So a true saving knowledge of sin is to be found only in Christ and him crucified.

Knowing ourselves in respect of righteousness. This is the second thing of which the Spirit of Christ convinces the world. All men know that God is a righteous God (*Gen. 18:25; Rom. 1:32; II Thess. 1:6; Hab. 1:13*). Because he is righteous 'the ungodly cannot stand before him in judgment' (*Psa. 1:5*). So man's great question is, 'How can a man make himself righteous to stand in the presence of a righteous God?'. Unable to discover a perfect righteousness for themselves, men 'through the fear of death, were all their lifetime subject to bondage' (*Heb. 2:15*). They are frightened to die lest their self-righteousness will not save them from death and destruction.

So man first looks to the law for a righteousness. The law says, 'Do this and live'. 'The doers of the law shall be justified.' 'If you will enter life, keep the commandments.' So men think that by keeping the law they will make themselves righteous before God.

But after great attempts to keep the law and failing, they come to the same conclusion as did Paul: 'By the works of the law, no flesh shall be justified'. Paul tells us that this happened with the Jews (*Rom. 9:31, 32*). They earnestly sought after righteousness by the law, but they failed to find it in that way. So Paul says, 'if there had been a law given which could have given life, then righteousness would have been by the law' (*Gal. 3:21*).

There are two reasons why man cannot work out for himself a righteousness by perfectly obeying the law. He has already sinned and the wages of sin is death (*Rom. 3:23; 6:23*). And even if all former debts should be blotted out, yet man is still unable to fulfil the law. 'By the works of the law, no flesh shall be justified.' Man's flesh, weakened by sin, cannot walk in perfect obedience to the law.

So, convinced of his utter inability to make himself righteous by the law, man turns to some other way by which he can please God. Papists turn to buying works of super-erogation and indulgences, to penances and to purgatory. This Paul calls a seeking for righteousness 'as it were by the works of the law' (*Rom. 9:32*). They did not try and obey the law itself, 'but as it were' by the works of the law, substituting one thing for another. 'By doing this,' says Paul, 'they proved themselves enemies to God's righteousness (*Rom. 10:3*). They were enemies to God's righteousness

[94]

because they tried to establish their own righteousness. And they tried to establish their own self-righteousness because they were ignorant of God's righteousness.

Self-righteous man is thus brought to see himself in two ways:

(1) He sees himself as a sinner condemned by God's law. Unless satisfaction is made for his sins, it is useless for him to think he can stand before the righteous and holy God.

(2) He sees himself as a creature bound to perfectly obey God's holy law.

Both these, sinful man is made to see he cannot do. He cannot make himself righteous by atoning for his sins, and he cannot make himself righteous by perfectly obeying God's law. It is the Holy Spirit's work to convince him of this. So being brought to the end of himself, he is ready to learn God's way of making him righteous, and this way can only be learned in Christ.

He learns that Christ has fully atoned for his sins. He learns that Christ has fully satisfied divine justice for his sins (*Rom. 3:24, 25; Isa. 53:6; Eph. 1:7; Rom. 8:32*). So in Christ alone is righteousness to be found.

So the soul can say, 'He has taken away the guilt of my sin by which I come short of the glory of God. The Word of God assures me that there is now no condemnation to those that are in Christ Jesus (*Rom. 8:1*). So being in Christ Jesus by faith, none can lay anything to my charge or condemn me (*Rom. 8:33, 34*). And as one who is in Christ by faith, conscience no longer condemns me for sin (*Heb. 10:2*).' This wisdom is hidden in Christ alone.

But it is not enough to say that we are not guilty. We must also be perfectly righteous. The law must be fulfilled by perfect obedience if we would enter into eternal life. And this is found only in Jesus (*Rom. 5:10*). His death reconciled us to God. Now we are saved by his life. The perfect actual obedience that Christ rendered on earth is that righteousness by which we are saved. His righteousness is imputed to me so that I am counted as having perfectly obeyed the law myself. This must be my righteousness if I would be found in Christ, not having my own righteousness which is of the law, but the righteousness which is of God by faith (*Phil. 3:9*).

'All the treasures of this wisdom of God's righteousness are hidden in Christ, who of God is made to us wisdom and righteousness' (*I Cor. 1:30*).

Knowing ourselves in respect of judgment. The true wisdom of this is also hidden in Christ Jesus. We are all to face God's judgment in the last day, and there are two things we need to know about it:

(1) We need to know the truth of this judgment to come. In Christ and by Christ, we are convinced of this judgment to come, and that in two ways:

(a) We are convinced of this judgment to come by Christ's death. God, in the death of Christ, punished and condemned sin in the flesh of his own Son, in the sight of men, angels and devils. This absolutely assures us of a righteous and universal judgment to come. The death of Christ is the greatest example of the last judgment. Those who know him to be the Son of God will not deny a judgment to come.

(b) We are convinced of this judgment to come by Christ's resurrection (*Acts 17:31*).

(2) We need to know how this judgment is to be carried out. It will be carried out by him who loved us and gave himself for us, who is himself the righteousness that he requires at our hands. It will be carried out by him who has been, in his person and grace, ways and worship, honoured by his servants, but reviled, despised and held in contempt by the men of the world. To the one he holds out unspeakable joy, but to the other, unspeakable terror.

This wisdom is also hidden in Christ. So in Christ we are made wise as to sin, righteousness and judgment.

A further part of our wisdom is to know how to walk with God. If we would walk with God, six things are necessary:

(1) If we would walk with God, it is necessary that we agree with him (*Amos 3:3*). By nature, God and man are enemies (*Rom. 8:7, 8*). Walking with God is the last thing an enemy of God seeks. Only in Christ can foolish men learn the wisdom of walking with God.

Christ takes away the cause of the enmity between God and man, which is sin and the curse of the law (*Dan. 9:24; Gal. 3:13*).

Christ has destroyed him who would continue the enmity between God and man (*Heb. 2:14; Col. 2:15*).

Christ made reconciliation for the sins of the people (*Heb. 2:17; II Cor. 5:19*). He reconciled God to man.

Christ reconciles man to God by slaying the enmity on our part (*Rom. 5:11; Eph. 2:18*). Only in Christ is this reconciliation to be found. Out of Christ, God is a consuming fire.

(2) If we would walk with God, it is necessary that we be friends of God. Strangers do not walk together. Not only must our enmity be taken away, but we must also know God as our friend. This also is hidden in Christ, and comes from him (*I John 5:20; John 1:18*). Only in Christ can we know God and know him as our friend and no longer our enemy.

(3) If we would walk with God, it is necessary that we walk with him in the way of holiness. This way is hidden in Christ and can only be learned from Christ (*Heb. 10:20; John 14:6; Isa. 35:8; 42:16*).

(4) If we would walk with God, it is necessary to be strong. We need strength to walk in the way of holiness. In ourselves we have no strength (*Rom. 5:6*). All strength comes from Christ (*Phil. 4:13*). Our sufficiency is in Christ (*II Cor. 3:5*). In Christ we are more than conquerors (*Rom. 8:37*). Any step

[97]

taken in this way without Christ is one step to hell. He takes us by the arm. He teaches us the way to go. He leads to perfection. So 'be strong in the Lord and in his almighty power' (*Eph. 6:10*).

(5) If we would walk with God, it is necessary to walk with confidence. We need confidence to walk with God, who is 'a consuming fire' (*Heb. 12:29*). Only in Christ have we boldness and confidence to walk with God (*Eph. 3:12*). This boldness comes from faith in Christ's blood (*Heb. 10:19*). Christ takes away the spirit of fear and bondage and gives us the Spirit of adoption, enabling us to cry 'Abba, Father' (*Rom. 8:15*). Now as there is no sin that God will more severely punish than any boldness to walk with him apart from Christ, so there is no grace more acceptable to him than boldness to walk with him in Christ through faith in the blood of Jesus.

(6) If we would walk with God, it is necessary to have the same purpose and aim as God. This also is to be found in Jesus. God's purpose is to glorify himself and none can aim at this purpose except those who are in Christ Jesus.

So the whole wisdom of our walking with God is hidden in Christ and comes to us from him alone.

11: *Consequences of Fellowship between Christ and his Saints*

When Christ gives himself to the soul, then he loves that soul forever. He 'loves them to the end' (*John 13:1*). And when the soul gives itself to Christ 'they love him in sincerity' (*Eph. 6:24*).

CHRIST TAKES GREAT DELIGHT IN HIS SAINTS (*Isa. 62:5*)

The delight of the bridegroom on his wedding day is the delight of his love for his bride. For Christ, every day we live is his wedding day. Christ so loves his people that he sings with joy over them (*Zeph. 3:17*). The thoughts of the fellowship he would have with his saints were the joy of his heart from eternity (*Prov. 8:31*).

The Father, from eternity, chose a people out of this sinful human race whom he intended to save. These he entrusted to Christ and appointed him to be their Saviour. Christ agreed to undertake their salvation and rejoiced at the thought of all the pleasure and delight that he would have in them when he would actually bring them into that loving fellowship with himself. From eternity, Christ took them into his care and rejoiced at the thought of saving them from eternal condemnation. Concerning his saints, Christ says, 'Here I will dwell and here I will make my home for ever'. Christ says this because he has chosen his saints as his temple. He will dwell in them because he delights in them. He takes them into an intimate fellowship with himself. As he is God, so his saints are his temple. As he is king, his saints are his subjects. As he is the head, so his saints are his body, his church. As he is the firstborn, he makes his saints his brothers. 'He is not ashamed to call them brethren.'

Christ so delights in his saints that he reveals his secrets to them. He also enables them to reveal the secrets of their hearts to him. It is only to a trusted friend that we will unburden our hearts. The greatest evidence that we have a delightful, loving fellowship with someone is that we share our most intimate secrets with that person. We will not keep them at a distance by talking of commonly known things.

Christ, then, reveals his mind to his saints and to them alone. He shares with them his mind, his loving counsels, his heartfelt thoughts and all his secret plans. He shares with them the ways of his grace, the workings of his Spirit, the rule of his sceptre and the obedience of the gospel for our eternal good (*Mal. 4:2; Luke 1:78; II Pet. 1:19; Psa. 25:14; John 15:14, 15*).

How does Christ reveal these things to us? He reveals them to us 'by his Spirit'. We have 'received the Spirit that we might know the things that are freely given to us by God'. Christ sends us his Spirit to make his mind known to us and to lead us into all truth. There is nothing in Christ's heart that he does not reveal to us. 'We have the mind of Christ' (*I Cor. 2:16*). Christ tells us all his love, his good will, the secrets of his covenant, the paths of obedience and the mystery of faith. But none of these things are revealed to unbelievers with whom he has no fellowship (*I Cor. 2:14*).

There is a great difference between understanding the doctrine of Scripture and truly knowing the mind of Christ (*I John. 2:27*). This, Christ's people have by a special anointing from Christ (*I John 2:20*).

What, then, are the things that Christ delights to reveal to his saints?

Christ delights to reveal himself to his saints (John 14:21). He will reveal himself in all his grace, desirableness and loveliness. He will reveal himself to them as Saviour, Redeemer and the chief among ten thousand. He will reveal himself as the pearl of great price. Others will see in him no beauty and nothing to desire in him. But to his saints, in whom is all his delight, he will show himself and all his glorious and excellent properties that they may see how lovely he is. From the world he will hide himself. But his saints, with open face, will see his beauty and his glory and be transformed into his glorious image by the Spirit of the Lord (*II Cor. 3:18*).

Christ delights to reveal his kingdom to his saints. His saints will be acquainted with the government of his Spirit in their hearts. They will understand his rule and his authority in his Word and among his churches. They will know more and more of the secrets of his kingdom whilst the world knows nothing of the secrets of the Lord.

Christ enables his saints to reveal their minds and souls to him that they might walk together in intimate love and friendship. Christ knows the minds of all (*John 2:25; Rev. 2:23*). But to know this truth will not avail us if we do not know how to open our hearts to him. This we do in prayer. To Christ, the prayers of his saints are like incense (*Rev. 8:3*).

If we would open our hearts to Christ, we need help to pray. This help we have by the Spirit of Jesus (*Rom. 8:26, 27*). All attempts at praying without the help of the Spirit working in us a prayerful spirit are of no avail and of no value. Christ greatly delights in the prayers of his saints when they truly open their hearts to him (*Song 2:14*). When the soul is driven to hide from Christ, then Christ calls it out and enables it to pray by giving it the help of his Spirit.

If we would open our hearts to Christ, we need a way by which to approach God with our desires. This way we have in Christ (*John 14:5, 6*). Adam at creation had a way open to God.

But this way has been shut up by sin and the sword of the law guards that way. But Jesus has 'consecrated a new and living way through the veil, that is to say, his flesh' (*Heb. 10:20*). This way is open to believers only.

If we would open our hearts to Christ, we need boldness to go to God. Out of Christ, souls are filled with terror at the thought of approaching God (*Isa. 33:14*). Sin fills them with shame and trembling. But believers now have 'boldness to enter into the holiest by the blood of Jesus' (*Heb. 10:19*). Only in Christ do we find boldness to approach the thrice-holy God.

So to encourage us to open our hearts to him, Christ has given us the help of his Spirit, himself as the way, and boldness to approach a reconciled God.

Now we must look at something of great importance. What is the difference between a true spiritual revealing of our minds to Christ, and praying merely because we think we ought to pray?

In true prayer, the Spirit of Christ reveals to us our own needs, so that we can take these needs to Christ (*Rom. 8:26*). For a soul to know its real needs and infirmities it needs the help of the Holy Spirit. The prayer of the one who has this help is more than half made before he begins to pray. His conscience, mind and spirit are aroused to bring his burden and unload it on Christ. He finds, not by a sense of guilt, but by a holy sense and weariness of sin, where he is dead, where dull and cold, where unbelieving, where tempted above his strength, and where the light of God's face is not seen. A sense of need is the spring of desire. Natural needs arouse natural desires. Spiritual needs arouse spiritual desires. So without the help of the Holy Spirit, there is neither desire nor prayer.

In true prayer, the Spirit of Christ helps us to express our desires in words. Expressing prayer in words is hard because our words do not fully express the deep desires within us. Therefore 'the Spirit makes intercession with sighs and groans that cannot be uttered'. Some men's words go beyond their hearts' desires. If their spirits came up to their expressions, all would be well. But the one who truly prays ends up dissatisfied with his prayers. He is dissatisfied because his prayers are not a work of righteousness to be trusted in. If God should mark what is wrong with his prayers, then he would fall in the day of judgment (*Isa. 64:6; Psa. 130:3*). He is dissatisfied also because his heart has not poured out adequately its holy desires and deepest needs, even though in Christ he may have found great relief and comfort. The more the saints speak to Christ, the more they find they have left much unspoken.

In true prayer, the Spirit of Christ helps the saints to pray according to the mind of God. They are guided by the Spirit to ask for those things which it is God's will they should desire and ask for. These are the things God knows are good for them in their present situation (*Rom. 8:28*).

There are many ways by which we may know when we pray according to the will of God, but I will show you only one. We know we are praying according to God's will when we ask for those things he has promised to give or do for us (*Psa. 119:4, 9*). It is possible to pray for what is in the promise but not according to the promise (*James 4:3*). Though we may ask for what has been promised, yet if we do not have the same idea as God as to why we should have it, we do not pray according to his will.

If we would pray for the things God has promised, we must see them as promised in Christ. We must see that our one hope of getting what is promised is only from the mediation and purchase of Christ. This is praying to the Father in Christ's name. God, as Father, gives the promise. Christ, by his death, has procured that promise for us. The Father puts the promise in Christ's hands and we must therefore get the promise from him.

[103]

If we would pray for the things God has promised, we must ask for that which he has promised for the same reason that God gave us the promise and not to spend it on satisfying our own lusts. When we ask pardon for sin, but secretly mean to continue in sin, we ask amiss to spend it on our lusts. The purpose of God's promises is that we may 'cleanse ourselves from all pollution of the flesh and spirit, perfecting holiness in the fear of God' (*II Cor. 7:1*).

THE SAINTS' DELIGHT IN CHRIST

Christ is their delight, their crown, their rejoicing, their life, food, health, strength, desire, righteousness, salvation and blessedness. Without Christ they have nothing. In Christ they shall find all things. Christ has, from the foundation of the world, been the hope, expectation, desire and delight of all believers. Adam was given the first promise of Christ (*Gen. 3:15*). Eve thought the promise was fulfilled in Cain (*Gen. 4:1*). Lamech thought Noah was the promised seed (*Gen. 5:29*). Abraham rejoiced to see the day of Christ and he saw it and was glad (*John. 8:56*). Jacob's faith in Christ is also seen (*Gen. 49:8, 9*). Simeon sums up the whole Old Testament faith in Christ (*Luke 2:30, 31*). The prophet Haggai tells us that Christ is 'the desire of all nations'. In the Song of Solomon, the Shulamite, symbolising the Church, tells us that she sits down under his shadow with great delight (*Song 2:3*).

This delight of the Shulamite is seen in her exceedingly great care to keep him with her always (*Song 2:7*). Having found sweet fellowship with Christ, she declares her delight in it and desires that it may be continued. Her great desire is that the daughters of Jerusalem, symbolising those outwardly professing to know Christ, may not disturb him or do anything that will cause him to depart from her. When once the soul of a believer has come into sweet and real fellowship with Christ, it watches carefully and guards all the ways by which sin might approach to disturb the enjoyment it has in its Lord and Saviour. A believer that has Christ in his arms is like one that has found great riches. He does everything in his power to prevent those riches from being taken away. So having Christ, in whom are hidden all the riches and treasures of God, will make men extra careful not to lose him. Carelessness concerning fellowship with Christ is evidence of a false heart.

This delight of the Shulamite is seen in her utmost impatience when he is absent, and by her desires for a nearer, more intimate relationship with him (*Song 8:6*).

The Jewish high priest spiritually represented the church before God. He had a breastplate which he wore on his heart (*Exod. 28:29*). On this the names of the children of Israel were engraved, and he bore them for a memorial before the Lord. Engraved stones were on his shoulders and on his arms (*Exod. 28:11, 12*). Now the seal on the heart signifies a close, inward, tender love and care of the image of the one loved. 'Set me,' says the Shulamite, 'as a seal on your heart' (*Song 8:6*). As if to say, 'Let me be constantly fixed in your most tender love. Let me always have a place in your heart. Let me be an engraving, a mighty impression of love upon your heart that will never be obliterated.' The soul is never satisfied with thoughts of Christ's love to it. It says, 'Set me as a seal on your arm'. The heart is the fountain of love, but it is hidden. The arm is the revelation and power of love. The Shulamite is clearly seeking continual care and protection from her beloved. She wants to have her name engraved on his arm. So Christ continually cares for the soul and has even engraved it on his arm (*Isa. 49:15, 16*). The Shulamite also desires that her beloved's power should be exalted in his care and protection of her. So Christ's exalted power is set to keep the soul secure in his love. Christ will not lose one soul whom he has loved from eternity.

The reason the Shulamite gives for her earnest prayer is that 'love is as strong as death, jealousy as cruel as the grave' or as 'hard as hell'. As if she said, 'I am not able to bear the tremendous love I have for you unless I may always have you with me and always have loving fellowship with you. My love will never be satisfied without this. My love is like the grave that still says, 'Give, give!'. Death is never satisfied. It is always crying, 'More, more!' If it has not all, it has nothing. Nor can death be resisted when its time has come. No ransom will be taken. So is my love. If I do not have the whole of your love, I have nothing. The whole world cannot satisfy my love and bribe me away from you. Also, I am not able to bear my jealous thoughts. I am afraid that you do not love me, that you have forsaken me. I know I do not deserve to be loved by you. These thoughts are hard as hell. They give no rest to my soul. If I do not find myself engraved on your heart and arm, I am like one that lies on a bed of coals.'

Doesn't this show the soul's great delight in Christ?

The Shulamite goes on to show her great delight in her beloved by her trouble and anxiety when she loses him or he leaves her. Men bewail the loss of that which they most treasure. The state of the Shulamite is seen by her frantic search for him in the streets of the city (*Song 3:1–3*). When darkness descends on the soul, then it knows that Christ is absent. But was the Shulamite happy with this situation? She is upon her bed taking her rest. But without Christ, there can be no rest or comfort. She gets up and seeks for her beloved.

Searching for Christ. When the soul realises that Christ is no longer present, then it begins to search itself to find out the cause of his absence. The soul calls itself to account for what it has done, how it behaved when Christ was present that caused him to leave. It asks itself, 'Why has Christ withdrawn himself? What have I done to drive him away? Have I been wandering after other lovers?'. And when the cause is known, the soul is aroused to wrath against itself.

The soul then begins to search the promises of the covenant where Christ is most clearly to be found. But they are to the soul like dead corpses. The soul does not know what to do. It has lost its greatest jewel and does not know where to look for it. In panic it searches everywhere. 'I sought him,' it says, 'but I did not find him.'

But the Shulamite does not give up. 'I will rise now and go about the city; in the streets and the squares I will seek the one I love' (*Song 3:2*).

She resolves to use every means. The believer seeks Christ in prayer, meditation, self-searching, as well as in the promises. The believer resolves to repent of his careless attitude to Christ and resolves to diligently seek him until he finds him.

The Shulamite leaves the house and goes about the city. The city symbolises the church, which is the city of God. The broad and narrow streets symbolise the paths and ordinances given to the church. The soul seeks him in prayer, preaching and the sacraments. But in all these things, Christ is not found. 'I sought him but I did not find him.' Beware, then, of losing Christ. It may cost you much bitter searching before you find him again.

The Shulamite in her search says, 'The watchmen who go about the city found me' (*Song 3:3*). The watchmen symbolise Christ's appointed ministers. In chapter 5:7, they turn persecutors. But here they do their best to help the Shulamite.

It is the duty of faithful ministers to take notice of poor, troubled, deserted souls and be willing to help them. When the Shulamite leaves them, she finds him whom her soul loved (*Song 3:4*). How she came to find him we are not told.

It often happens that when all our searchings have not brought us to him we are left to wait silently for him and to walk humbly until he appears.

When she found him, she 'held him and would not let him go' (*Song 3:4*). This clearly shows the soul's delight in Christ and all that belongs to Christ.

Christ greatly delights in his people and they greatly delight in him. This is the first consequence arising from the loving fellowship between Christ and his saints.

12: *Further Consequences of Fellowship with Christ*

Having brought his saints into a loving fellowship with himself, Christ highly values them. They are his precious jewels (*Mal. 3:17*).

All that Christ did or does as Mediator was for their sakes.

For their sakes he was 'made flesh' (*Heb. 2:14, 16*). He set more value on his saints than on angels. 'He did not take on him the nature of angels.'

For their sakes he became poor, that through his poverty, they might be eternally rich (*II Cor. 8:9*).

For their sakes he became a servant (*Phil. 2:6, 7*). As a servant, he fulfilled all righteousness, endured all manner of persecutions and hardships and did all manner of good to men (*Heb. 5:7, 8*).

For their sakes he became obedient to the death of the cross (*Phil. 2:8*). The curse of the law was in his death (*Gal. 3:13*). The loss of God's presence was in his death (*Psa. 22:1*). The wrath of God was in his death (*II Cor. 5:21*). 'Greater love has no man than this, that a man lay down his life for his friends' (*John 15:13*). 'God demonstrates his own love towards us, in that while we were yet sinners Christ died for us' (*Rom. 5:8*).

For a man to part with his glory, his riches, his life, his sense of the love of God in order to suffer loss, shame, wrath, being cursed and even death for another is clear evidence that he greatly values that person for whom he is willing to undergo such suffering. But this is exactly what Christ did for his saints. So in this way he showed how greatly he loved them (*Heb. 12:2; Eph. 5:25, 26*).

Christ values his saints above all others. All the world is nothing to him in comparison to his saints. They are his garden. The rest of the world is a dry desert (*Song 4:12*). They are his inheritance, the rest his enemies, of no worth in his eyes (*Isa. 43:3, 4*). He rules, governs and disposes of all nations and their interests for the good of his saints (*Amos 9:9*). Nations are blessed for their sake (*Gen. 12:3; Mic. 5:7, 8*). Nations are destroyed for their sake (*Isa. 34:8; 61:2; 63:4*). And nations are preserved to try them or rejected for their cruelty to them. They will receive from Christ their final doom according to their behaviour towards those despised ones (*Matt. 25:41–46*). Angels are appointed to minister to his saints (*Heb. 1:14*).

There is not the meanest, the weakest, the poorest believer on earth that Christ does not value more highly than all the world besides.

THE SAINTS GREATLY VALUE CHRIST

Believers also value Christ and that above all the world and all the things in the world (*Psa. 73:25*).

Saints value Christ above all other things and persons. Moses valued the reproach of Christ more than all the treasures of Egypt (*Heb. 11:26*). The very first lesson the gospel teaches believers is to despise all things for Christ. 'Give away all. Take up the cross and follow me' were the words with which Christ tested his disciples of old. And if there is not the same heart and mind in us, we are none of his.

Saints value Christ above their lives (*Acts 20:24*). Saints of old rejoiced when whipped, scourged and put to shame for his sake (*Acts 5:41; Heb. 11*).

Saints value Christ above all spiritual excellences and all other righteousness whatever (*Phil 3:7, 8*). The Holy Spirit speaks of Jesus Christ as the wisdom of God, the eternal wisdom of the Father (*Prov. 3:13–15*). He and his ways are better than silver and gold and all other desirable riches whatever. The glory of Christ's deity, the excellence of his person, and his wonderful works greatly delight the eyes and hearts of his saints.

All that Christ parted with, all that he did, all that he suffered were all done because he loved and valued his saints.

Christ so values his saints that he will never ever lose one of them (*John 17:11; 10:28, 29*).

Saints, on the other hand, rejoice to part with all things for Christ and his sake, that they might enjoy him for ever. But one thing saints will never do and that is part with Christ.

CHRIST'S HELP FOR HIS PEOPLE (*Eph. 5:29*)

Christ has a fellow-feeling for his saints. He suffers in all their troubles. He feels for his saints in all their temptations and in all their afflictions.

He sympathises with them in all their temptations (*Heb. 4:15*). He was tempted as we are. So Christ shows compassion to his saints in all their infirmities, temptations and spiritual weaknesses.

Christ pities his saints and suffers in their sufferings. 'He who touches them touches the apple of his eye' (*Zech. 2:8*).

Christ greatly supports and helps his saints (*Isa. 40:11*). Here we see Christ's tenderness, compassion and caring nature. He is as tender and caring as is a faithful shepherd. So all Christ's saints may take this as a sure rule, both in their temptations and in their afflictions, that they shall always have Christ's support and strength (*I Cor. 10:13; Heb. 2:18*).

The following are some examples of how Christ helps his saints.

Christ sometimes strengthens the soul against the sin that assaults it. He did this with Joseph (*Gen. 39:9*). So Christ strengthens and fortifies the hearts of his saints with abundant grace to resist the temptations to sin.

Christ sometimes, by some strong impulse of actual grace, removes the soul from the very borders of sin. He did this with David (*I Sam. 24:4–6*).

Christ sometimes takes away the temptation itself when it grows so strong and violent that the poor soul does not know what to do (*II Pet. 2:9*). He knows how to deliver the godly out of temptation. Christ comes in the storm and says, 'Peace, be still'.

Christ sometimes gives more grace as temptations grow and increase. He did this with Paul (*II Cor. 12:9*).

Christ sometimes gives wisdom to make a right, holy and spiritual use of all temptations. This is what James tells us to do (*James 1:2*). Peter tells us that sometimes it is necessary to be left in many temptations (*I Pet. 1:6*).

Christ supports the soul, when it is at any time more or less overcome by temptations, with mercy and pardon, so that it will not sink utterly under the burden.

Christ shows his compassion to his people in all their afflictions (*Isa. 63:9; Col. 1:24*). His compassion is revealed in two ways. He intercedes with his Father for them (*Zech. 1:12*). And he avenges his elect on those who cause them to suffer (*Isa. 34:8; Luke 18:7*).

Christ avenges his elect in time, upon persons, kingdoms, nations and countries. Pharaoh is a good example of such vengeance (*Exod. 9:16*). He was a great opposer of God and so was made a great example of God's vengeance. God also avenges his saints by pouring out the vials of his wrath on the whole anti-christian world. He will judge the enemies of his people with eternal vengeance (*Matt. 25:41–46; II Thess. 1:6; Jude 15*).

SAINTS ARE FAITHFUL TO CHRIST

Paul, writing to the Christians in Corinth, tells them that he has betrothed them to one husband that he may present them a chaste virgin to Christ (*II Cor. 11:2, 3*).

There are three things in which faithfulness to Christ lies.

Faithfulness to Christ means that we do not take into our hearts or value something or someone as equal to or better than Christ to do for us what we initially received Christ for. The Galatians failed to be faithful to Christ. They had received Christ for life and justification, and him only. But they were bewitched by the Judaisers and instead of trusting Christ only for life and justification, they looked also to the law to do this, and valued the law equally with Christ. Faithful believers receive Christ for their righteousness and salvation before God. They look to him alone to supply all their needs. They will not now receive any other thing along with Christ.

We receive Christ for our acceptance with God. Now all that competes with Christ for our hearts must be our own good works and efforts for a righteousness to commend us to God. Now this must be either before we receive Christ or after. All our good works and endeavours to please God before receiving Christ, Paul rejects as rubbish (*Phil. 3:8–10*). He shows that all his faith is in Christ and his righteousness alone to make us acceptable with God. But what about the works we do after receiving Christ? These are indeed acceptable to God. He is pleased that we walk in them. But they are of no value in God's eyes in making us righteous (*Eph. 2:8–10*). The works we do after believing, those which we were created in Christ Jesus to do, those that God ordained that believers 'should walk in', are rejected as far as our justification and acceptance with God are concerned. To trust in our own good works as well as in Christ for our salvation is to be a spiritual adulterer. To faithful believers, Christ is made by God 'righteousness' and they will trust nothing else but Christ for righteousness.

Wherever that question is to be answered, 'With what shall I come before the Lord, and appear before the high God?', the faithful believer never says, 'This or that I will do' or 'Here and there I will watch and amend my ways'. Instead, he cries out, 'In the Lord Jesus I have righteousness; all my desire is to be found in him, not having my own righteousness'.

Faithful believers cherish the Holy Spirit, the Comforter that Christ sends to us, to abide with us as his representative in us (John 16:7). Christ gives the Holy Spirit to us that he might abide with us for ever. So whatever is done to any of Christ's people is done to him, because it is done to them in whom Christ dwells by his Spirit. Saints show their love to Christ by doing their best, by all means in their power, not to grieve his Holy Spirit (*Eph. 4:30*).

Christ sent his Spirit to believers, firstly for their sanctification, and secondly for their comfort. So we can grieve the Holy Spirit by resisting his work of holiness in us and leading unholy, polluted, defiled lives. Faithful believers aim to be holy, as God is holy, and to walk even as Christ walked.

We can also grieve the Holy Spirit in his work as Comforter. As Comforter, the Spirit seals us, anoints us, establishes us and gives us peace and joy. We grieve the Holy Spirit, firstly by placing our comforts and joys in other things and not being filled with joy in the Holy Spirit. When our delights and comforts lie in earthly things, we are not fit for fellowship with Christ. May not his Spirit say, 'Why do I still abide with these poor souls? I provide them with unspeakable and glorious joys, but they refuse them, preferring things that perish. I provide them with spiritual, eternal, abiding comforts and it is all rejected for a thing of nought.' This Christ cannot bear. So faithful believers get their hearts crucified to the world and the things of the world. And when they have lost their better joys, they cry out to Christ, 'Oh restore to us the joys of your Spirit!'

The Holy Spirit is also grieved when, through darkness and unbelief, we will not and do not receive those comforts which he brings us and which he eagerly waits for us to receive.

Faithful believers worship Christ according to his directions and use only those means which he has appointed. Unfaithfulness in this, Christ calls 'adultery' and 'whoredom'. He is 'a jealous God'. False worship is called 'fornication'. The church that leads others to false worship is called the 'mother of harlots'. Faithful believers therefore endeavour to keep their hearts faithful in his ordinances, institutions and worship.

Believers will receive nothing, practise nothing, recognise nothing in the worship of Christ but only that which he has appointed. God never allowed the will of the creature to decide how best to worship God. Worshipping God in ways not appointed by him is severely forbidden. God asks, 'Who has required these things at your hand?' And again, 'In vain do you worship me, teaching for doctrines the traditions of men'.

The principle that the church has power to institute and appoint any thing or ceremony belonging to the worship of God other than what Christ himself has instituted is the cause of all the horrible superstitions and idolatry, of all the confusion, blood, persecution and wars that have arisen in the Christian world. The purpose of a great part of the book of Revelation is to show this truth. When the Spirit of God in prayer is derided, the powerful preaching of the gospel is despised, the Sabbath decried, holiness persecuted, then Jesus Christ is deposed from the sole privilege and power of law-making in his church, the true husband is thrust aside and adulterers of his betrothed embraced. Taskmasters are appointed in and over his house – taskmasters that he never gave to his church (*Eph. 4:11*). A ceremonious, pompous, outward show, drawn from pagan, judaic and antichristian sources is introduced, of all of which there is not one word, not one jot or tittle in the whole book of God.

But faithful believers will admit nothing, practise nothing in the worship of God, private or public, but what Christ has ordained. Unless it comes in his name with 'Thus says the Lord Jesus', they will not even listen to an angel from heaven. They know the apostles themselves would teach the church only what Christ commanded them (*Matt. 28:20*).

Faithful believers embrace, receive and practise everything that the Lord Christ has appointed. They seek diligently to find out what is in his mind and what he wants done and they will do nothing that is not pleasing to him.

PROOF OF CHRIST'S LOVE

Christ shows and proves his love to his saints in richly providing for all their needs (John 1:16). All that Christ does for us he does abundantly. There is no niggardliness on Christ's part to his saints (*Rom. 5:20*). Where sin abounded, grace abounded much more. If grace abounds more than sin, it is abundant grace indeed. He answers our prayers 'exceedingly abundantly above all that we ask or think' (*Eph. 3:20*). He abundantly pardons (*Isa. 55:7*). He sheds the spirit on us abundantly (*Titus 3:6*). We receive 'abundant grace' (*Rom. 5:17*). He 'abounds to us in all wisdom and prudence' (*Eph. 1:8*). The great sin of believers is that they do not make as much use of Christ's bounty as they might. Every day we ought to take from him mercy in abundance. Supplies from Christ do not fail. But our faith fails in receiving them.

In view, then, of all Christ's goodness to us, what is our duty to him?

Our first duty to Christ is to practise holiness in the power of the Spirit. The most holy person is the one most obedient to Christ.

Believers obey Christ as the author of their faith and obedience (*Heb. 12:1, 2; Phil. 1:29*). Christ by his Spirit works obedience in them.

Believers obey Christ as the one by whom our obedience is accepted by God. Believers know all their duties are weak, imperfect and unable to abide in God's presence. Therefore they look to Christ as the one who bears the iniquity of their holy things, who adds incense to their prayers, gathers out all the weeds from their duties and makes them acceptable to God.

Believers obey Christ as the one who has renewed the commands of God to them, placing them under a mighty obligation to obedience (*II Cor. 5:14, 15*).

Believers obey Christ as the one who is God, equal with the Father, to whom all honour and obedience are due (*Rev. 5:13*).

In all their obedience, saints have a special regard to their dear Lord Jesus. He is continually in their thoughts. His love to them, his life for them, his death for them, all his mercy and all his kindness constrains them to live to him.

Our second duty to Christ is to abound in fruits of holiness. As he abounds richly towards us, so he requires us to abound richly to him in all grateful obedience (*I Cor. 15:58*).

This is but a little glimpse of that communion which we enjoy with Christ.

13: *Communion with Christ in Purchased Grace*

Purchased grace is all that righteousness and grace which Christ has procured or wrought for us and of which he makes us partakers.

This purchased grace has been wrought for us by Christ's obedience, by his sufferings and by his continual intercession.

Purchased grace is the grace of justification or acceptance with God.

Purchased grace is the grace of sanctification or holiness before God.

Purchased grace is the grace of privilege.

That we have communion with Christ in this purchased grace is clearly seen in that there is almost nothing that Christ has done, but we are said to have done it with him (*Gal. 2:20; II Tim. 2:11; Col. 3:3; Rom. 6:4; Col. 2:12; 3:1; Eph. 2:5, 6*).

Christ purchased this grace of justification, sanctification and privilege by his perfect obedience to the whole will of God. Christ might have been perfectly holy by obedience to the law of creation, the moral law, as the angels were. Nothing more could have been required of him as a mere man walking with God. But Christ submitted himself to every law and ordinance which sin had made necessary and which, because he was sinless, he could not have been subject to. He did this 'to fulfil all righteousness' (*Matt. 3:15*).

Christ's obedience was done as Mediator (*Heb. 5:8*). It was his obedience in his sufferings which gave life to his death (*Phil. 2:8*).

Christ was obedient to death, for by his death he made his

soul an offering for sin (*Isa. 53:10; John 17:19; Heb. 9:14; Eph. 5:2*).

The righteousness of Christ as Mediator in his human nature was the absolute, complete, exact conformity of Christ's soul to the will, mind or law of God. In himself he was perfectly and always righteous. This righteousness which the man Christ Jesus had was because of the grace of union, the union of the divine with the human nature. So as our high priest, he was holy, harmless, undefiled and separate from sinners (*Heb. 7:26*). He was the Lamb of God without spot or blemish (*I Pet. 1:19*).

The actual obedience of Christ was his willing, cheerful, obedient carrying out of every duty or command that God required of man as man and man as a sinner.

Christ fulfilled all that was required of us by virtue of any law. He fulfilled all that the law of nature required in our state of innocence. He fulfilled the moral law, the ceremonial law and all judicial laws. Christ did it all. So he 'was made under the law' (*Gal. 4:4*).

Christ also fulfilled the spiritual law as Mediator. These concerned himself only and are not for our imitation (*e.g. John 10:18*). He obeyed the command of his Father to lay down his life and to take it again. He prayed for those who put him to death (*Luke 23:34*). He prayed for his elect only (*John 17:9*).

COMMUNION WITH CHRIST IN THIS GRACE OF RIGHTEOUSNESS

It was necessary that we should have a Mediator that was both God and man in one person, and a Mediator that was perfectly holy. So Christ alone was fit to be our high priest and Mediator.

All that Christ was enabled to do in obedience was by his inherent righteousness and the Spirit of God (*Isa. 61:1*).

Christ, being perfectly righteous, was a fit sacrifice and offering for sin without his active obedience. Therefore there must be some other reason for his life of active obedience.

Christ's obedience to the special commands of God given to him as Mediator is not imputed to us. By obedience to this law, Christ bought for us all the good things we need for salvation.

Christ also obeyed that law which God required of us. Some believe this obedience was preparatory to his blood-shedding and oblation. His death, they consider, is the sole cause of our justification, the whole righteousness which is imputed to us. His obedience is purely an act of obedience which is no cause of our justification. This is wrong.

Christ's obedience even to the death of the cross was united to that death which was part of his state of humiliation and so it is imputed to us along with his death.

Christ's obedience for us is reckoned to us by God's grace, and on account of this we are accepted as righteous before him.

Christ's obedience yielded to the law in general was done as Mediator. He was incarnate in order to be Mediator (*Heb. 2:14; Gal. 4:4*).

Whatever Christ did as Mediator he did for those whose Mediator he was or in whose place and for whose good he carried out the office of Mediator before God (*Rom. 8:3, 4*). What his people could not do because of sin, Christ did for them. He did it so that the righteousness of the law might be fulfilled in us.

The whole purpose of Christ's obedience cannot be said to be merely to fit him for his death and oblation, because he was in himself the Lamb without spot or blemish and therefore quite fit to be the sacrifice for sin. He did not need to make himself a fit sacrifice for sin by a course of obedience.

If Christ's obedience is not imputed to us, having been done on our behalf, then there is no reason why he should have lived so long in the world as he did in perfect obedience to all the laws of God. Had he died earlier, his death would have been a sufficient atonement in itself for our sins.

If Christ's perfect obedience had not been for us, then all that would have been required of him was obedience to the law of nature, the only law to which he, a sinless man, could have been subject. His obedience to this law was a voluntary act of his in becoming man.

Christ's obedience cannot be reckoned among his sufferings but is clearly distinct from his sufferings. Doing is one thing. Suffering is quite another.

WHAT WAS INTENDED BY CHRIST'S OBEDIENCE

Christ's obedient life showed his willing submission to, and his complete fulfilling of, every law of God that any of the saints were obliged to obey. It is true that every act of Christ's obedience from the blood of his circumcision to the blood of the cross was attended with suffering so that his whole life might be seen as one long death. But yet, when we see his willingness and obedience in it all, then this willingness and obedience is distinguished from his sufferings as such, and so his willingness and obedience are known as his active righteousness.

Christ obeyed, not for himself, but for us and in our place, as Paul tells us (*Gal. 4:4, 5*). From this text of Scripture we learn that Christ was both made of a woman and made under the law; that is, he obeyed the law for us. We were under the law, not only under its condemnation, but also bound to perfectly obey it (*Gal. 4:21*). The Galatians had no desire to be under the penalty of the law, but only to be under the obligation to obey the law. So if Christ were not incarnate, nor made under the law for himself and did not obey it for himself and his own justification, then he did it all for us and for our good and our justification. Let us now see how this helps us in our acceptance with God.

HOW CHRIST'S OBEDIENCE HELPS US

Christ's complete obedience to the law is reckoned to us. Death is the reward of sin, and so we cannot be freed from death, but by the death of Christ (*Heb. 2:14, 15*). Man cannot be freed from the condemnation of death until he has done all the law requires (*Matt. 19:17*). As man cannot keep all the commandments, it must be done for him by a surety. Christ not only obeyed all the commandments on behalf of man, but he also bore the penalty of death. But though we are freed from the penalty of death, we are still bound to obey the law. Yet that obedience is not to gain acceptance with God, but rather it is an expression of gratitude to God for our deliverance from death.

Why did Christ die? He died because the law demanded the death of a sinner, and Christ was the surety for sinners.

How, then, are we delivered from death? We are delivered from death as a punishment. We must still die, but now death is the last battle with the effects of sin, and it is the way to the Father's personal presence.

How did Christ yield perfect obedience to the law? He did it in response to the covenant of works imposed on mankind: 'Do this and live'. Christ perfectly obeyed in the strength of the grace he had received. He obeyed so that he could procure life for man. He obeyed in order to fulfil the covenant God made with man.

Are we, then, freed from obedience? Yes. We are freed from obeying the law in our own strength, and we are freed from obeying it in order to obtain everlasting life. To say that we must still obey in order to obtain everlasting life is to say we are still under the terms of the old covenant. We are not freed from obedience as a way of walking with God, but we are freed from obedience as a means of making ourselves good enough to come to God.

By Christ's obedience to the law we are made righteous (*Rom. 5:18, 19*). His obedience is reckoned to us for righteousness.

Christ's obedience was active because Adam's disobedience was active. Adam's disobedience was an active transgression of the law, and so Christ's obedience was an active obedience to the law (*Matt. 5.17*). There is no such thing as 'passive' obedience. Obeying is doing in which suffering has no place.

The righteousness we receive must be that righteousness which we would have had if we had obeyed the whole law (*Phil. 3:9*). This is the obedience of Christ to the law. So he is 'made to us righteousness' (*I Cor. 1:30*).

The outcome of Christ's death is based on reconciliation. Reconciliation is a slaying of the enmity and restoring us to that condition of peace and friendship in which Adam was before his fall.

But is there no more to be done? Even though Adam in his state of innocence was not under wrath, yet he was to obey if he would enter into life. But is there something more to be done even after the slaying of the enmity and the bringing in of reconciliation? Yes. 'Being reconciled by his death', we are saved by that perfect obedience that Christ yielded to the law during his life. There is a clear mention made of reconciliation through sin not being imputed to us (*Psa. 32:1; Luke 1:77; Rom. 3:25; II Cor. 5:19*). There is also a clear mention of justification through righteousness being imputed (*Jer. 23:6; Rom. 4:5; I Cor. 1:30*). This justification, through righteousness being imputed, we have by the life of Christ.

This is illustrated by Joshua, the high priest, clothed in filthy rags (*Zech. 3:3–5*). Two things are clearly taught in these verses respecting our free acceptance before God. Firstly, the guilt of our sin, our filthy rags, is taken away. This is done by the death of Christ. The fruit of this is remission of sins. Secondly, there is a change of raiment, symbolising the imputation of Christ's righteousness to us. The fruit of this is a right to eternal life. So the Holy Spirit calls this change of raiment 'the garments of salvation' and 'the robe of righteousness' (*Isa. 61:10*). This is only made ours by the obedience of Christ, as the other was by his death.

Objection. 'But if this is so, then surely we are as righteous as Christ himself, being righteous with his righteousness.'

Answer. First, there is a great difference. This righteousness which is imputed to us was inherent in Christ and so truly his own. This righteousness of Christ's was reckoned or imputed to us, or freely given to us, and we are made righteous with that which is not ours. But secondly, the truth is that Christ was not righteous with that righteousness for the benefit of himself, but for us. So that there can be no comparison. We are righteous with his complete and perfect righteousness which he wrought for us. By the death of Christ, the guilt and punishment of sin is taken away from us. By his obedience imputed to us, we have a complete and perfect righteousness.

COMMUNION WITH CHRIST IN HIS DEATH AND SELF-OFFERING

He lived for us and he died for us. He was ours in all he did and in all he suffered.

The death of Christ was a price paid (I Cor. 6:20; I Pet. 1:18, 19; Matt. 20:28; I Tim. 2:6)

Christ paid the price for our redemption. Redemption is the deliverance of anyone from bondage or captivity and the miseries accompanying that condition by the paying of a price or ransom. The Redeemer pays the price to the one who holds authority over the captive.

In general, redemption is a deliverance. So Christ is called 'the deliverer' (*Rom. 11:26*). He gave himself to 'deliver us' (*Gal. 1:4*). He is 'Jesus who delivers us from the wrath to come' (*I Thess. 1:10*).

Redemption is the delivery of one from bondage or captivity. Without Christ, we are all prisoners and captives, 'bound in prison' (*Isa. 61:1*). We are prisoners 'sitting in darkness, in the prison house' (*Isa. 42:7; 49:9*). We are 'prisoners in the pit where there is no water' (*Zech. 9:11*). We are 'the captives of the mighty, and the prey of the terrible' (*Isa. 49:25*). We are under 'a captivity that must be led captive' (*Psa. 68:18*). This puts us 'in bondage' (*Heb. 2:15*).

The one who commits us to prison and into bondage is God himself. To him we owe 'our debts' (*Matt. 6:12; 18:23-27*). We have offended him (*Psa. 51:4*). God is the judge and lawgiver (*James 4:12*). To sin is to rebel against God. He shuts up men under the power of disobedience (*Rom. 11:32*). It is God who will cast both the bodies and souls of all the impenitent into hell fire (*Matt. 10:28*). To his wrath all men are subject and we all lie under his wrath by the sentence of the law which is our prison (*John 3:36*).

The miseries that accompany this condition are numberless. Bondage to Satan, sin and the world is the sum of them. From all this bondage we are delivered by the death of Christ as a price or ransom (*Col. 1:13, 14; Tit. 2:14; I Pet. 1:18, 19; Heb. 9:15; Gal. 4:5*).

From all this bondage and all these miseries we are delivered by the payment of the price mentioned into the hand of God, by whose supreme authority we are held captive under the sentence of the law. We are delivered from the debt due to the great householder (*Matt. 18:23,*

24). We are delivered also from the penalty of sin and from God's curse and wrath (*Rev. 1:5*).

This redemption by Christ, the Holy Spirit frequently mentions (*Rom. 3:24, 25; I Cor. 6:20; I Pet. 1:18; Matt. 20:28; I Tim. 2:6; Eph. 1:7; Col. 1:13; Gal. 3:13*).

The death of Christ was a sacrifice. Christ's death was a sacrifice also. He had a body prepared for him (*Heb. 10:5*). In this body, Christ was to accomplish what the Old Testament sacrifices and burnt offerings symbolised. And that body, Christ offered (*Heb. 10:10*). His whole human nature is included in the term 'body', for 'his soul' also was made 'an offering for sin' (*Isa. 53:10*). So he is said to offer himself (*Eph. 5:2; Heb. 1:3; 9:26*). He gave himself a sacrifice to God (*Rom. 5:10; Heb. 2:17*). So Christ's death as a sacrifice was also for atonement and reconciliation.

Sin had broken the friendship that was originally between God and man (*Isa. 63:10*). So God's wrath now abides on us (*John 3:36*). We are, by nature, under his condemnation (*Eph. 2:3*). This is taken away by the death of Christ as the sacrifice for sin (*Dan. 9:24; Rom. 5:10*). So by Christ's death, we receive 'the reconciliation' (*Rom. 5:11*). Paul said, 'God was in Christ reconciling the world to himself, not imputing their trespasses to them' (*II Cor. 5:19*).(See also *Eph. 2:12–16.*)

The death of Christ was a punishment. Christ's death was also a punishment. He was punished instead of sinners (*Isa. 53:5*). God laid all our iniquities, that is, the punishment of them, on Christ (*v. 6*). He 'bore the sins of many' (*v. 12*). He 'bore our sins in his own body on the tree' (*I Pet. 2:24*). He 'who knew no sin was made sin for us' (*II Cor. 5:21*). The following verses describe what it is to bear sin: Deut. 19:15; 20:17; Numb. 14:33; Ezek. 18:20.

When Christ bore our punishment, he gave full satisfaction to God, who was offended and because of that offence inflicted the punishment. Justice can desire no more than 'an eye for an eye and a tooth for a tooth'. Thus, the exact punishment we deserved, Jesus voluntarily took upon himself when he undertook to be our Mediator. His substituting himself in our place, which God allowed, was the means by which satisfaction for our sins was made to God.

So if we would have communion with Christ, we are to hold communion not only in his life of obedience for us but also in his death for us as a price, a sacrificial offering and a punishment.

CHRIST'S INTERCESSION

The Lord Christ goes further still. He does not leave us merely as forgiven and redeemed, but carries on his work to the utmost. 'He died for our sins and rose again for our justification' (*Rom. 4:25*). Christ rose again to carry on the complete work of purchased grace by his intercession (*Heb. 7:25*).

Christ's intercession is his 'appearing in the presence of God for us' (*Heb. 9:24*). The high priest, having offered the great offering for the expiation of sin, carried the blood of the sacrifice into the most holy place. The holy place was where God was represented. So to perfect the atonement he made for himself and the people, the high priest carried the blood into the most holy place. In the same way, the Lord Christ, having offered himself as a sacrifice to God, and now sprinkled with his own blood, appears in the presence of God, as it were, to remind God of the promise he had made to Christ, the promise to redeem sinners by his blood, and that he also promised to give these redeemed sinners all the good things purchased by the blood of Christ.

Christ, by his intercession, procures the Holy Spirit for us, and he gives us his assurance that he will do this for us (*John 14:16*).

14: *The Nature of the Grace which Christ Purchased*

Christ has purchased for us three great blessings. He has purchased for us: acceptance with God, sanctification from God and many great privileges with and before God.

Acceptance with God. Out of Christ, we are in a state of alienation from God. Sin separates us from God. So the first work of purchased grace is to restore us to acceptance with God. Christ bought us acceptance with God by removing the cause of the enmity between God and us, and by giving us that which it was necessary for us to have in order that we might be accepted by God.

By his death on the cross, Christ removed sin and its guilt. 'He who knew no sin was made sin for us' (*II Cor. 5:21*). And he is made 'to us, righteousness' (*I Cor. 1:30*).

But this does not complete our acceptance with God. The old quarrel may be laid aside, and yet no new friendship begun. We may not be sinners, and yet not be righteous enough to have a right to the kingdom of heaven. Adam had no right to life because he was innocent. He must 'do this' and then he shall 'live'. He must not only have a negative righteousness, not being guilty of anything, but he must also have a positive righteousness by doing all things.

So the second thing we need in order to be completely accepted by God is that we not only do not have sin imputed to us, but that we also have a perfect righteousness reckoned to us. Now this we have in Christ's life of perfect obedience. This is our righteousness before God. By his obedience we are 'made righteous' (*Rom. 5:19*).

So with sin removed and righteousness bestowed, we are

accepted by God for ever. This is the first part of purchased grace in which the saints have communion with Jesus Christ.

Sanctification from God. Christ not only makes us accepted with God, but also acceptable to God. He not only purchases love for his saints, but also makes them lovely. He came, not by blood only, but by water and blood. He not only justifies his saints from the guilt of sin but also sanctifies and washes them from the filth of sin. The first is from his life and death as a propitiatory sacrifice, and the second from his death as a purchase and his life as an example (*Heb. 9:14; Eph. 5:26, 27*). So Christ removes the defilement of sin and bestows cleanness.

By the grace of sanctification, our natures are continually cleansed. We are naturally unclean and defiled, and that continually (*Job 14:4; John 3:6*). It is in the pollution of our blood that we are born (*Ezek. 16*). We are wholly defiled and polluted. The grace of sanctification, purchased by the blood of Christ, removes the defilement of our natures (*I Cor. 6:11; Titus 3:3–5*). By this cleansing, the soul is made fair and beautiful in the sight of God. Though the sin that defiles remains, yet its continual defilement is taken away.

By the grace of sanctification, all the pollutions of our actual transgressions are taken away. Every actual sin defiles. Our own clothes make us loathsome (*Job 9:31*). A spot, a stain, rust, wrinkle, filth, blood accompanies every sin. Now 'the blood of Jesus Christ cleanses us from all sin' (*I John 1:7*). Besides the defilement of our natures which he purges, he takes away the defilement of our actual persons caused by our foolishness. 'By one offering he perfected for ever those that are sanctified.' By himself, he 'purged our sins' before he sat down at the right hand of the majesty on high (*Heb. 1:3*).

By the grace of sanctification, our best duties are cleansed from defilement. Even our very best duties are defiled (*Isa. 64:6*). Self, unbelief and formality insinuate themselves into all that we do. God has promised that the saints' good works shall follow them. In fact, if our good works were tested and weighed in the balance of the sanctuary, it would be just as well if they were buried for ever. But the Lord Christ, as our high priest, bears the iniquity and the guilt of our best works and washes away all their filth and defilement. He is like a refiner's fire to purge both the sons of Levi and their offerings, adding sweet incense to them so that they may be accepted (*Mal. 3:3*). Whatever is of the Spirit himself, or of grace, will remain. Whatever is of self, flesh and unbelief, that is wood, hay and stubble. These he burns up. The good works of the saints shall meet them one day with a changed face, so that even they will not recognise them. That which seemed to the saints to be black, deformed and defiled shall appear beautiful and glorious. Saints shall not be afraid of their works, but rejoice in them.

This cleansing of our natures, persons and duties has its whole foundation in the death of Christ. So our washing and purifying, our cleansing and purging is brought about by his blood shed and sprinkled on us and our works. The sprinkling of the blood of Christ comes from the Holy Spirit, whom Christ promised to us as purchased by him for us. The Holy Spirit is the pure water by which we are sprinkled from all our sins. He is that Spirit of judgment and burning that takes away the filth and blood of the daughters of Zion (*Isa. 4:4*).

The blood of Christ not only removes the defilement of sin, but also gives purity.

The Spirit of holiness is given to us to dwell in us. Christ is made to us sanctification (*I Cor. 1:30*). How? By procuring for us the Spirit of sanctification. Our renewing is of the Holy Spirit, who is shed on us by Christ alone (*Titus 3:6*). The first and chief gift of sanctification that we receive from Christ is the indwelling of the Spirit and our being guided by him (*Rom. 8*).

Habitual grace is given to us as a principle of grace opposed to the principle of lust that is in us by nature. This is the grace that dwells in us. In the understanding, it is light. In the will, it is obedience. In the affections, it is love. But it is all one principle, all one grace.

Actual ability to perform every spiritual duty is given to us. Without Christ, we can do nothing (*John 15:5*). Believers continually depend on Christ for new influences of grace or for supplies of strength from the Spirit. For every new act, believers need new grace. Christ must work in us to will and to do for his good pleasure (*Phil. 2:13*). So purchased grace gives us the Spirit of holiness, habitual grace and actual ability to carry out every spiritual duty.

Privileges with and from God. The first privilege we have is that of adoption, the Spirit of adoption. And having been adopted, we enter into all the benefits of the gospel which only the saints have a right to. But these we shall deal with later under 'Communion with the Holy Spirit'.

These are the things, then, that we have by purchased grace. We have acceptance, holiness and adoption and the inheritance of sons. That is glory indeed!

15: *Communion with Christ in Acceptance with God*

Believers enjoy fellowship with Christ in acceptance with God, holiness, and in the privileges grace brings them.

On Christ's part, only two things are required if we are to have fellowship with him in our acceptance with God.

Firstly, what Christ did, he did for us and not for himself. He was made 'under the law' so that we might receive the adoption of sons (*Gal. 4:4, 5*). He sanctified himself so that we 'may be sanctified through the truth' (*John 17:19*).

His sufferings were not for himself (*Dan. 9:26*). The main difference between Christ and the Jewish high priests is that when they made their solemn offerings, they offered first for themselves and then for the people. But Jesus Christ offered only for others. He had no sin and could make no sacrifice for his own sin. He 'tasted death for everyone' (*Heb. 2:9*). He 'gave his life a ransom for many' (*Matt. 20:28*). 'The iniquity of us all' was laid on him (*Isa. 53:6*). (See also *I Pet. 2:24; Eph. 5:25; Gal. 2:20; Rom. 4:25; Rev. 1:5, 6; Titus 2:14; I Tim. 2:6; Isa. 53:12*.) He suffered for us, 'the just for the unjust that he might bring us to God'.

Secondly, Christ provides and purchases for us a perfect righteousness in order that we might be accepted with God.

There are many promises declared to us in the gospel. (See *Matt. 11:28; Rom. 10:4*.) These declared promises are very precious, but the Lord Christ knows that the outward letter, though mightily preached, will not enable any to receive him for righteousness and salvation. A law is established in the gospel that whoever receives it shall be accepted and saved.

But Christ knows that none, of themselves, will receive the gospel.

Therefore he sends them his Holy Spirit to quicken them (*John 6:63*). By his Holy Spirit, he causes those who are 'dead to hear his voice' (*John 5:25*). So by his Spirit, Christ works in them all that is required to make them partakers of his righteousness and accepted with God.

Christ lived and died in order to work out a perfect righteousness for his people. He then tells them what he has done and finally he actually gives this righteousness to them and regards them as if they had worked out that righteousness themselves, so that by this righteousness they will be perfectly accepted with the Father.

So for us to be accepted by the Father, two things are necessary. Firstly, that satisfaction is made for our disobedience, and secondly, that the righteous demands of the law be fulfilled. Both these were fully and perfectly done for us by Christ (*II Cor. 3:21; Gal. 3:13; Rom. 8:33, 34; I Pet. 2:24; Rom. 5: 18, 19*). Our sins were imputed to Christ so that they will not be imputed to us. Instead, Christ's righteousness is imputed to us so that we might be accepted by God.

Knowing these things, we now need to know how to have fellowship with Christ in this grace of acceptance with God and how we may keep alive our acceptance with God. Without this, life is hell, for there can be no peace and joy.

But first we must deal with two objections:

'If the elect have absolution, reconciliation and freedom by the death, blood and cross of Christ, why is it, then, that they are not all actually absolved at the death of Christ or, at least, as soon as they are born? Why do many of them live for a long time under the wrath of God in this world, as unbelievers, under the sentence and condemning power of the law? (*John 3:36*). Why are they not immediately freed upon the payment of the price, reconciliation having already been made for them? And also, if the obedience of Christ is imputed to us and that is our righteousness before God, then why do we need to obey? Is not all our praying, labouring, watching, fasting, giving alms and all fruits of holiness, flowing from a pure heart and leading to a useful life, all completely redundant? And who, then, will or need take care to be holy, humble, righteous, meek, self-controlled, patient, good, peaceable, or to abound in good works in the world?'.

The answer to these objections lies in the work of reconciling us to God which Christ undertook. He was set up to be the representative of all those for whom he died to reconcile them to God. So he is the 'Mediator between God and man' (*I Tim. 2:5*). He 'gave himself a ransom for all' (*v. 6*). He is the 'surety of a better covenant' (*Heb. 7:22*). He was, to all intents and purposes, the righteousness of his spiritual seed, as Adam was sin to his natural seed (*Rom. 5:15–19*).

His being the representative of his people arose from the covenant entered into by himself with his father for this very purpose. The terms of the covenant are clear (*Isa. 53:3*). It is summed up in Isaiah 40:7, 8; Hebrews 10:8–10. The Father became his God, which is a covenant expression (*Psa. 89:26; Heb. 1:5; Psa. 22:1; 40:8; 45:7; Rev. 3:12; Mic. 5:4*). So Christ was set up by his Father for this work (*Isa. 42:1, 6; 49:9; Mal. 3:1; Zech. 13:7; John 3:16; I Tim. 1:15*). Thus, the 'counsel of peace' was set up 'between them both' that is, the Father and the Son (*Zech. 6:13*). The Son rejoices from eternity in the thought of undertaking this work (*Prov. 8:22–30*).

His being the representative of his people arose also from the sovereign choice of the elect by the Father and his giving them to Jesus Christ in this covenant to be redeemed and reconciled to himself (*John 17:6*). They were God's by eternal election and he gave them to Christ to be redeemed.

So even before their calling or their believing, Christ calls them his 'sheep' (*John 10:15, 16*). So we are said to be 'chosen in Christ before the foundation of the world' (*Eph. 1:4*).

His being the representative of his people arose from his undertaking to suffer the punishment due to them and to do what was to be done by them so that they might be delivered, reconciled and accepted with God. And he undertakes to give to the Father, without the loss of any, all he had received from the Father (*John 17:2, 12; 6:37, 39*).

His being the representative of his people arose from his receiving on their behalf and for them, all the promises concerning all the mercies, grace, good things and privileges which they were to receive as the result of his work of reconciling them to God. So eternal life is said to be given to us 'before the world began' (*II Tim. 1:9*). This was given to us in Christ, our appointed head, Mediator and representative.

As the representative of his people and having undertaken everything for their salvation he was, as such, acquitted, absolved, justified and freed from all and every one of their sins that were charged upon him. So all the saints of the Old Testament were saved by his blood no less than we. Christ was declared to have fulfilled all that he had undertaken when he was 'declared to be the Son of God with power, by the resurrection from the dead' (*Rom. 1:4*). He was 'justified' (*I Tim. 3:16*). God made Christ under the law on behalf of those who were under the law (*Gal. 4:4*). On their behalf, to pay the punishment for their sins, God made Christ 'to be sin' (*II Cor. 5:21*). So God gave justice and law and all the punishments that man deserved, power to satisfy their demands on Christ (*Isa. 53:6*). So upon his undergoing all that which was required of him, God frees him from the pains and power of death, accepts him and is well pleased with him for what he has done. God now pronounces Christ free from the obligation that was upon him. God also gave Christ a promise of all the good things he purchased by his death, and which his soul desired. So Christ, on our behalf and as our surety, was acquitted and absolved, because he had answered for the whole debt that was laid upon him to pay. He had made satisfaction for all the injury we had done. Now a general pardon is held out to all, to be claimed in the way God has appointed.

Christ, therefore, having fulfilled all that was laid on him, and because the terms of the covenant had been fulfilled, it was right that God should bestow on all those on whose behalf Christ stood, the fruits of his death in his work of reconciliation with God (*Rom. 5:8–11*). As Christ was acquitted on their behalf, so his people are also acquitted (*II Cor. 5:21; Gal. 3:13; I Pet. 2:21, 24*).

So being thus acquitted because of being in the covenant of the Mediator, believers are said to be circumcised with him, to die with him, to be buried with him, to rise with him, to sit with him in heavenly places. It was right that they should be personally acquitted in the covenant of grace. It was determined by the Father, Son and Holy Spirit that they should be actually and personally delivered from the sentence and curse of the law, and in such a way as might lead to the praise of the glorious grace of God (*Eph. 1:5–7*). God's purpose was that we should be adopted as his children. We were to be brought to this state by Jesus Christ. The special way of bringing it about is by the redemption that is in his blood. The whole reason for this is for the praise of his glorious grace.

But until such time as they are actually delivered, a time determined by God in their several generations, they are personally under the curse of the law from which they shall certainly be delivered. They are under the law, not with the intention of being punished, but as it is a means appointed to help them to come to faith in Christ and so to acceptance with

God. When this is accomplished, then their whole obligation to the law for justification ceases. Their condition was that they could not fulfil the perfect obedience required by the law, and so by the law they are led to faith in Christ and by Christ to love the law and its obedience, to the praise of the glorious grace of God.

The whole purpose of grace is to glorify the whole Trinity, and the way this is done is by reaching up to the Father's love through the work of the Spirit and the blood of the Son. Divine love begins with the Father, is carried on by the Son and then communicated to us by the Spirit. The Father purposes, the Son purchases and the Holy Spirit effectively brings it to pass. So we are brought by the work of the Spirit to faith in the blood of Christ, by which we are accepted by the Father.

This, then, is how we are brought to acceptance with the Father, for the glory of God through Christ.

The Holy Spirit is glorified by being given to us to quicken us, convert us and to work faith in us (*Rom. 8:11; Eph. 1:19, 20*). This is according to all the promises of the covenant (*Isa. 4:4, 5; Ezek. 11:19; 36:26*).

The Son is glorified by this work of the Holy Spirit in us, for by it we come to trust in his blood shed for us and receive all the benefits of that shed blood, which includes the work of the Holy Spirit in us.

The Father is glorified when we are accepted by him, justified, freed from guilt, pardoned and have 'peace with God' (*Rom. 5:1*). 'Through Christ we have access by one Spirit to the Father' (*Eph. 2:17*). So the Father, the Son and the Holy Spirit are glorified in our justification and acceptance with God. The Father is glorified in his free love. The Son is glorified in his full purchase. The Holy Spirit is glorified in his effectual working.

All this grace, in all its parts, is no less fully procured for us, no less freely bestowed on us for Christ's sake, than it would have been if all of us, immediately on Christ's death, had been translated into heaven. Only, the reason why we are delivered and freed in the way we are is that the whole Trinity may be glorified. This sufficiently answers the first objection. Though our reconciliation with God is fully and completely purchased by the death of Christ, and the ways and means by which we enter into that reconciliation, yet we are brought into the actual enjoyment of it by the way mentioned above, for the praise of the glorious grace of God.

The answer to the second objection is that Christ's obedience imputed to us and our obedience done to God have two different functions. Christ's obedience imputed to us is so that we might be counted righteous before God and so be justified. But our obedience is not the righteousness by which we are accepted by God and justified, but it is that for which God has created us and which we do out of love and gratitude to him for his grace (*Eph. 2:8–10*).

Our obedience is 'the workmanship of God', wrought in us by full and effectual grace. God has ordained that we should walk in this obedience. This is a sufficient reason why we yield obedience to God.

Our wholehearted obedience and good works are indispensably necessary, from the sovereign appointment and will of God, Father, Son and Holy Spirit (*I Thess. 4:3*). It is the will of the Father (*Eph. 2:10*). It is the will of the Son (*John 15:16*). It is the will of the Holy Spirit. He appoints men to the great work of preaching the gospel (*Acts 13:2*). In sinning, we sin against the Holy Spirit.

Our holiness, that is, our obedience and works of righteousness, is one chief and special way by which God is glorified in our salvation.

It is the whole reason why the Father chose us (*Eph. 1:4; Isa. 4:3, 4; II Thess. 2:13*). It is this love of the Father that is the motive to holiness (*I John 4:8–10*). It is why the Son loved us and gave himself to redeem us (*Eph. 5:25–27; II Cor. 5:15; Rom. 6:11*). It is why the Holy Spirit does his work of love in us. He prepares us for obedience (*Titus 3:5; Gal. 5:22, 23*).

Obedience is also necessary to bring glory and honour to God (*Mal. 1:6*). The Father is glorified by our obedience (*Matt. 5:16*). The Son is glorified by our obedience (*John 5:23; 14:1; 17:10*). The Holy Spirit is glorified by our obedience and is grieved by our disobedience (*Eph. 4:30*). He dwells in us as his own temple, which is not to be defiled.

It is to our honour that we should obey, for we are called to be like God (*I Pet. 1:16; Matt. 5:48; Eph. 4:23, 24*). By our obedience, we have fellowship with God and so experience the peace of God in our hearts (*I John. 1:7, 3; Isa. 57:20, 21*). By our obedience, we become useful to God and man. Fruitless branches are cut off and burned. By obedience, we convict the world and stop their mouths from speaking evil of us (*I Pet. 3:16; John 17:23*).

One day the saints will judge the world. How? Their good works, their righteousness, their holiness shall be seen by all the world and the righteousness of God's judgments against the wicked will be revealed. 'See,' says Christ, 'these are they who are mine, whom you so despised and abhorred. Now see them. See their works. This is what they did while you wallowed in your abominations' (*Matt. 25:42, 43*).

By our obedience, others may be converted (*I Pet. 2:12; Matt. 5:16; I Pet. 3:1, 2*). Our obedience often benefits others, just as ten good men would have kept Sodom from judgment. Holiness makes a man a good man and useful to all. Others eat of the fruits of the Spirit that he continually bears.

Obedience is necessary for the state and condition of justified persons. We are received and accepted into friendship with a holy God, a God who is of purer eyes than to behold iniquity, who hates every unclean thing. Should we not be holy who are admitted into his presence and walk in his sight?

We have in us a new creature (*II Cor. 5:17*). This new creature is fed, cherished, nourished, kept alive by the fruits of holiness. Why has God given us new hearts and new natures? Is it in order that we should murder them? Are we to stifle the creature that is found in us whilst it is still in the womb? Should we give it to the old man to be devoured?

Obedience is necessary because of the place that holiness has in the covenant. God has purposed that holiness shall be the way to that eternal life which is his gift by Jesus Christ to us. But as eternal life is a gift, so also it is a reward and God is the rewarder of our obedience. Though our obedience is not the means by which we are justified, yet it is the way appointed by God for us to walk in to obtain salvation. And therefore, he that has the hope of eternal life in him purifies himself as Christ is pure, and none shall come to eternal life who does not walk in obedience, for without holiness no-one shall see the Lord.

Obedience is also a testimony and pledge of our adoption as children of God, a sign and evidence of grace and of our acceptance with God. Obedience is the best way of showing our gratitude to God for His grace.

Having therefore shown what Christ has done so that we might have fellowship with him, and having answered these two objections, it remains now only to show what is required of us to complete that fellowship with Christ.

We have communion with Christ when we heartily approve of this righteousness as purchased by him so that we might be accepted by God

To come to such a hearty approval of Christ's righteousness we need first of all to be aware that we need a righteousness with which to appear before God. If God is holy and righteous and of purer eyes than to look at iniquity, we must have a righteousness with which we are able to stand before him.

We will only approve of Christ's righteousness when we are convinced that our righteousness has been weighed in the balances and found wanting. The Jews made the mistake of trusting in their own righteousness (*Rom. 9:31, 32*). And so they were rejected (*Rom. 10:1–4*). (See Paul's judgment of man's righteousness in *Phil. 3:8–10*.) God declares that 'there is none righteous, no not one'. Isaiah declares that 'our righteousnesses are like filthy rags' (*Isa. 64:6*).

He who has fellowship with Christ approves of, values and rejoices in his righteousness by which he is accepted by God (*Isa. 44:24*). This is the pearl of great price (*Matt. 13:45, 46*).

When the righteousness of Christ is first revealed to a sinner as the only way to be accepted by God, he is amazed and full of wonder and rejoices greatly. So he heartily approves of this righteousness because it reveals the glory of the wisdom of God (*I Cor. 1:21*). He sees what darkness he was in. He looked into himself and found only sin, horror, fear and tremblings. He looked up and saw nothing but wrath, curses and vengeance. He saw that God was holy and righteous and that no unclean thing could abide with him. He saw that he was a poor, vile, unclean and sinful creature and he could not see how a holy God and a sinful creature could be reconciled. But in the righteousness of Christ, a world of wisdom is opened, dispelling all difficulties and darkness and revealing how reconciliation could actually happen (*Rom. 11:33; Col. 2:3*).

What grace is revealed in this righteousness of Christ! The sinner does not have to earn it. God everywhere assures us that this righteousness is of grace (*Rom. 11:6; Eph. 2:7–9*). It is given to us by grace. It is from the riches of grace and kindness that this righteousness has been provided. So believers rejoice in this righteousness because it is ours by grace only.

Believers approve of and rejoice in this righteousness because it brings great peace and assurance to their souls. They remember what fears they had before. But now 'being justified by faith, they have peace with God' (*Rom. 5:1*). All is quiet and still. Not only is the storm over, but they are safely anchored in the harbour. They have abiding peace with God. So we have that wonderful description of Christ given to us in Isaiah (*Isa. 32:2*). The soul, through Christ, is at perfect peace with God (*Isa. 26:3; Psa. 4:6–8*). So the souls of believers glorify the Lord Christ because they can come boldly to God with confidence, peace, joy and assurance. They can call him Father. They can strengthen themselves in his love. They can walk in peace and live without fear. Once they ran from him for fear. Now they approach him with love, joy and peace.

Believers heartily approve of Christ's righteousness because it greatly exalts and honours the Lord Jesus whom they love. Believers desire nothing more than that Jesus Christ be honoured and glorified to the utmost so that in all things he might have the pre-eminence. And how can we honour him more than to know that he is made to us by God 'wisdom and righteousness'? (*I Cor. 1:30*).

Believers know that because Christ worked out our acceptance with God, he is honoured by God his Father (*Phil. 2:7–11*). Because he was obedient to the death of the cross, God has highly exalted him and given him a name above every name.

Christ is also honoured by all the angels in heaven, who not only bow down and desire to look into the mystery of the cross, but also worship and praise him always (*I Pet. 1:12; Rev. 5:11–14*). They praise him as the Lamb that was slain. So the saints rejoice to know that all the angels of God, the whole host of heaven who never sinned, continually rejoice and give praise and honour to the Lord Jesus, for his bringing them to peace and favour with God.

Christ is honoured by his saints all over the world. If they do not, who will? If believers do not honour him as they honour the Father, they are of all men the most unworthy. But we are shown what believers do (*Rev. 1:5, 6; 5:8–10*). The great, solemn worship of the Christian church lies in honouring and glorifying the Lord Jesus (*Phil. 3:8; Song 5:9–16*).

Believers heartily approve of this righteousness, this way of being accepted by God, because it brings glory to God. When they were under the guilt of sin, they were puzzled as to how they could be saved and God's justice, faithfulness and truth glorified. Believers see that, by this righteousness, all the properties of God are greatly glorified in the pardon, justification and acceptance of sinners.

This is, then, the first way by which saints hold daily fellowship with the Lord Jesus.

Believers continually keep alive in their hearts a sense of the guilt and evil of sin, even when they are fully assured of their acceptance with God. A sense of pardon takes away the horror and fear, but not a due sense of the guilt of sin.

David said, 'My sin is ever before me'. Believers set sin before them, not to terrify themselves but so that they are always aware of the evil of it.

Believers gather up in their thoughts the sins for which they have not made a particular reckoning with God in Christ. There is nothing more dreadful than for a man to have sin look him in the face and speak words of terror to him and to be able either to forget them or to put off dealing with them. Believers gather up their sins and lay them in the balance of the law. They see and consider their weight of evil and what they deserve. Then they seriously consider – and, by faith, conquer all objections to the contrary – that Jesus Christ, by his Father's will and appointment, had really suffered the punishment that was due to those sins (*Isa. 53:6; II Cor. 5:21*). Christ has certainly and really answered the justice of God for our sins. This is the believer's full assurance of faith.

Believers hear the voice of Christ calling them to come to him with their burdens (*Matt. 11:28*). So they come to him and lay their guilt upon him. They lay down their sins at the cross of Christ and he bears them on his shoulders. This is faith's great and bold confidence in the grace, faithfulness and truth of God. They stand by the cross and say, 'He was bruised for my sins, and wounded for my transgressions, and the chastisement of my peace was upon him. He was made sin for me. So he is able to bear my sins. He calls me to lay the burden of them on him.' This is the believer's daily work. This is what it means to know Christ crucified.

Having given up their sins to Christ by faith, and by faith seeing God laying them all on Christ, believers draw near and take from him that righteousness which he has wrought for them, so fulfilling what Paul taught (*II Cor. 5:21*).

Objection. But surely this can never be acceptable to Jesus Christ. Shall we daily come to him with our filth, our guilt, our sins? Will he not tell us to keep them ourselves? Shall we always be giving him our sins and taking his righteousness?

Answer. There is nothing that Jesus Christ is more delighted with than that his saints should always hold communion with him by giving him their sins and receiving his righteousness. This greatly honours him and gives him the glory that is his due. What great dishonour we do to Christ to try and get rid of our sins in any other way. 'Lord, this is your work. This is what you came into the world to do. You call for my burden which is too heavy for me to carry. Take it, blessed Redeemer, and give me your righteousness.' Then Christ is honoured. The glory of his mediation is given to him when we walk with him in this way.

This greatly endears the souls of the saints to the Lord Jesus and constrains them to value him highly. 'I have been with the Lord Jesus. I have left the burden of my sins with him. He has given me his righteousness and in this righteousness I can come with boldness to God. I was dead and am alive, for he died for me. I was cursed and now am blessed, for he was made a curse for me. I was troubled but have peace, for the chastisement of my peace was upon him. I did not know what to do, nor where to take my sorrow. But by him I have joy unspeakable and full of glory. If I do not love him, delight in him, obey him, live to him, die for him, I am worse than the devils in hell.' It is Christ's great aim in this world to be esteemed highly by his people. And how could he be more highly esteemed than to be acknowledged as the one who takes our sins and gives us his righteousness?

Objection. If this is so, why do we need to repent and amend our ways? Why not go on sinning, so that grace may abound?

Answer. I judge no-one. But this I must say, I do not understand how a man could make such an objection in cold blood. Can such a person know anything of true fellowship with Jesus Christ?

Communion with Christ produces repentance. When a person really sees the vileness of sin and what it cost Christ to bear it away, will he still want to continue in sin?

Communion with Christ produces obedience. 'If Christ is so glorified and honoured by taking our sins, the more we bring to him, the more he will be glorified.' A man could not suppose that this objection would be made, but that the Holy Spirit, who knows what is in man, has made it for them in their name (*Rom. 6:1–3*). If the gospel is properly preached, the objection 'shall we continue in sin that grace may abound?' will always be raised. But Paul says, 'God forbid!' – and then explains why not (*Rom. 6*).

How, then, should we practise this duty? By faith.

Faith exercises itself in this duty by meditation. The heart continually thinks of Christ, and what he has done and wants us to do.

Faith exercises itself in this duty by clinging to the promises in which the excellence, fulness and completeness of the righteousness of Christ are declared and held out to us.

Faith exercises itself in this duty by prayer. By prayer, we lay our sins on Jesus and receive his righteousness.

So this is how we have fellowship with Christ in the grace of acceptance with God.

16: *Communion with Christ in Holiness*

Now we must ask: How do we hold communion with Christ in holiness as well as in righteousness? If we would have fellowship with Christ in holiness, we must realise that there are several works of Christ necessary to bring us to holiness.

The first work of Christ necessary to bring us to holiness is his work of intercession. Christ intercedes with the Father, on the strength of his mediatorial work, that he would give the Holy Spirit to his people. The Holy Spirit was promised in the Old Testament (*Ezek. 11:19; 36:27; Jer. 32:39, 40*). Christ is the Mediator and 'surety of this new covenant' (*Heb. 7:22; 9:15*). As Mediator, he both satisfied for sin and procured the promise. He procures all the love and kindness which are the fruits of the covenant, he himself being the original promise of the covenant (*Gen. 3:15*). This covenant was 'ordered in all things and made sure' (*II Sam. 23:5*). In this covenant, he is to have the pre-eminence in all things (*Col. 1:18*). This was the compact and agreement made with him (*Isa. 53:12*). All the promises and benefits of the covenant were purchased by him. Therefore Christ intercedes with the Father on our behalf for the promised Spirit. Therefore he tells his disciples that he will not pray the Father for his love to be poured out on them, because the eternal love of the Father is not the fruit but the source of the purchase. The Spirit is the fruit of the Father's love. 'For that,' says Christ, 'I will pray the Father.' And what Christ as Mediator asks the Father to give us, that is what he has purchased for us, being promised to him on condition that he undertook to do the will of God (*Psa. 2:8; Isa. 53:12; Psa. 40:8–12*). So the first thing to be considered in our communion with Christ in holiness is that he intercedes with the Father for the promised Spirit of sanctification and holiness, that that Spirit may be given to us as a fruit of Christ's death for us. This, faith considers, takes hold of and meditates on.

The second work of Christ necessary to bring us to holiness is the receiving of the Spirit from the Father and sending him into the hearts of his saints, there to dwell in his place, and to do all things for them and in them which he himself has to do in them. This is the second thing that faith looks to in Christ. Faith does not only look for the initial coming of the Spirit to dwell in us, but also for the continual workings of the Spirit both in his works of grace and in his loving gifts. So it is Christ who sends the Comforter to us from the Father (*John 15:26*). Christ also shows us how he will send the Spirit. He will give the Spirit all the things he intends to give to his people. 'He,' says Christ of the Spirit, 'shall take of mine, those things which belong to me as Mediator and which I purchased by my life and death, and give it to you.' This is the second thing that Christ does and which faith takes hold of.

The third work of Christ necessary to bring us to holiness is that by his Spirit he imparts a new, gracious, spiritual life, or principle, created and bestowed on the soul by which the soul is changed in all its faculties and desires. The soul is filled and enabled to obey, and to receive every divine truth presented to it according to the mind of God. For instance, the mind can discern spiritual things in a spiritual manner because it has been 'illuminated by the Spirit'. Faith embraces Christ for righteousness and salvation as he is held out to us in the promises of the gospel. When faith rests in God and in Christ with delight, desire and satisfaction, it is called love. This new life was purchased for us by Christ and is actually communicated to us by Christ (*Phil. 1:29; Eph. 1:3; John 17:17; 1:16*).

The Father actually invests Christ with all the grace which, by agreement, he had purchased and which is necessary for bringing his many sons to glory (*Col. 1:19*). He was invested with a fulness of that grace which is needful for his people. Christ himself calls this the 'power of giving eternal life to his elect' (*John 17:2*).

Being actually invested with this power, privilege and fulness, he gives the Spirit the right to take of this fulness and to give it to us (*John 16:15*).

How we hold communion with the Lord Christ in these things

In the work of communicating the Spirit to our souls, raising them from death to life, we have no kind of fellowship with Christ, but only what lies in a passive reception of that life-giving, quickening Spirit and power. We were but dead bones on which the wind blew and made them live (*Ezek. 37*). We were like Lazarus in the grave. Christ called and we came out because his call was accompanied with life and power.

But once we have been brought from death to life and have received the gift of the Spirit, then we have communion with Christ in holiness. How we do this shall now be shown.

Faith continually looks at Christ as the great Joseph who has power and authority over all the granaries of the kingdom of heaven committed to him. It has pleased the Father to put all things into his hand as the head of all things (*Eph. 1:10*).

All that we need in order to be spiritually purified, spiritually cleansed and spiritually sanctified is to be found in Christ (*Heb. 9:13, 14*). His blood purges us from the works that we are driven to do by a guilty conscience or out of fear of what others might think if we do not do them, so that we might joyfully serve the living God. So Christ's blood is called 'a fountain for sin and uncleanness' (*Zech. 13:1*). It is 'a fountain opened', ready, prepared and effective because poured out, instituted and appointed for cleansing. The saints see that, in themselves, they are still exceedingly defiled. To have a sight of the defilements of sin is a greater spiritual insight than only to have the sense of the guilt of sin. A sense of guilt follows every conviction. But an awareness of sin's defilement only comes from an insight into the purity and holiness of God. Saints know also that no unclean thing shall enter the kingdom of God or have a place in the new Jerusalem, because God is of purer eyes than to behold iniquity and cannot look with pleasure at sin. Saints cannot endure having a good look at themselves, so how will they dare to appear before God? How or with what will they cleanse themselves? (*Jer. 2:22*). Only the blood of Christ cleanses from all sin (*I John 1:7*). It is the blood of Christ which cleanses from every spot and stain and which makes us holy and without blemish and fit to stand in the presence of God (*Eph. 5:26, 27*). Believers exercise their faith by thinking much about this. Here faith gets new life and new strength when a sense of vileness has overwhelmed it. Here is a fountain opened. Draw near and see its beauty, purity and effectiveness. One moment's communion with Christ by faith in this matter of cleansing is more effective to the purging of the soul and to growing in grace than the utmost efforts made by self.

Believers see the blood of Christ as the blood of sprinkling. Coming to 'Jesus, the Mediator of the new covenant', they come to 'the blood of sprinkling' (*Heb. 12:24*). Just seeing the blood of Christ as shed will not take away the pollution of sin. There is not only a 'shedding of blood' without which there is no remission of sins, but there is also a 'sprinkling of the blood' without which there is no purification (*Heb. 9:19–23*). In these verses, the blood of Christ is first compared to the blood of the sacrifices which were offered, and then to the blood that was sprinkled for purification and holiness. And we are told how the sprinkling was done. It was by dipping hyssop in the blood of the sacrifice and sprinkling it on the things and persons to be purified (*Exod. 12:7*). So David, aware of the pollution of sin, prays that he may be 'purged with hyssop' (*Psa. 51:7; Lev. 14:16; Numb. 19:18*).

Now this bunch of hyssop, in which the blood of purification was prepared for the sprinkling of the unclean, symbolises the free promises of Christ. The cleansing power of the blood of Christ lies in the promises, as the blood of sacrifices lay in the hyssop ready to be sprinkled on them that drew near. Therefore Paul argues from the receiving of the promise to the holiness and purity of the whole person (*II Cor. 7:1*). This, then, is what the saints do. By faith, they see the blood of Christ enshrined in the promise ready to be sprinkled on the soul for its purification. In this way, the 'blood of Christ cleanses from all sin' (*I John 1:7*). This purifying blood is made ready and prepared, but it waits to be applied to the soul. Though Christ has shed his blood for purification, cleansing and sanctification, while it remains in the bunch of hyssop in the promises, the soul is still not actually sprinkled. Only as the soul receives the promises by faith is the blood actually sprinkled and the soul purified.

So believers look on Christ as the only one who gives the Spirit and the one who gives all grace necessary for sanctification and holiness. Believers take it for granted that Christ will make good all that he has purchased for our sanctification, purification and glorification. Believers know that this is actually to be accomplished by the Spirit according to the innumerable promises given for that purpose. Christ is to sprinkle his blood upon sinful souls. He is to create holiness in our souls. He is to be a well of water in the souls of his saints, springing up to everlasting life. So believers look by faith to Jesus, expecting him to give the

Holy Spirit to work holiness in them according to the promises, and so become actual partakers of this grace. This is their way. This is their communion with Christ. This is the life of faith as it reaches out to take hold of grace and holiness. Blessed is the soul that is gripped by this truth (*Jer. 17.8*).

The natural man tries to spin out a web of holiness from his own fleshly efforts. Such men begin with great determination and follow this with vows, duties, resolutions and self-denials. In this way, they continue for a while, their hypocrisy, for the most part, ending in apostasy.

The saints of God, on the other hand, as they begin to walk with God, realise their need of these things.

Saints see their need of the Spirit of holiness to dwell in them.

Saints see their need of a habit of holiness to be infused into them.

Saints see their need of actual assistance to enable them to do the good works which God had planned for them to do.

Saints know that if these three things are lacking, they can never, with all their might, power and efforts, do one act of holiness before the Lord. They know that of themselves they are not sufficient for these things. They know that without Christ they can do nothing. Therefore they look to Jesus, and this is their communion with him in their life of sanctification and holiness.

17: *Communion with Christ in Privileges*

The third thing in which we have communion with Christ is in the grace of our privileges before God. All our spiritual privileges arise from one source, our adoption as children of God.

'Beloved, now we are the sons of God' (*I John 3:2*). This is our great privilege. Our adoption has its source in the love of the Father (*I John 3:1*). But by whom do we receive this honour? By Jesus Christ (*John 1:12*). He was appointed to be the firstborn among many brethren (*Rom. 8:29*). He takes us to be his brethren (*Heb. 2:11*). God is our Father because he is the Father of Christ. We are Christ's brethren, therefore his Father is our Father.

Adoption is the authoritative transfer of a believer, by Jesus Christ, from the family of the world and Satan into the family of God with his being admitted into all the privileges and advantages of that family

The person to be adopted must be actually, and of his own right, of another family than that into which he is to be adopted.

The person to be adopted must have no right whatever of his own to be taken into the other family.

The person to be adopted must be taken out of his natural family, and by an authoritative, legal transaction, be put into the other family. No person has the right to adopt when and whom they would. It must be done by the authority of a sovereign power.

The person to be adopted must be freed from all the

[153]

obligations that held him to his own family, otherwise he cannot in any way be useful or serviceable to the family which adopts him. He cannot serve two masters, much less two fathers.

The person to be adopted must, by virtue of his adoption, be admitted into all the rights, privileges, advantages and title to the whole inheritance of the family into which he is adopted in as full a manner as if he had been born into that family.

All these things are to be found in the adoption of believers. They are 'by nature, the children of wrath' (*Eph. 2:3*). They are born into the family of the world and of Satan, who is the god of this world (*Col. 1:13*). Whatever is to be inherited in that family, whether wrath, curses, death or hell, they have a right to it. Neither can they, of themselves, free themselves from this family. A strong man armed keeps them in subjection. They are of the cursed family of sin and Satan.

There is another family into which they are to be adopted, and to which they have no right or title. This is that family in heaven and earth which is called after the name of Christ, the great family of God (*Eph. 3:15*). God has a house and family for his children. Some he maintains on the riches of his grace and some he entertains with the fulness of his glory. In this family, all the sons and daughters of God live, and live largely on the riches of his grace. To this family they have no right or title. They are wholly alienated from it and can lay no claims to anything in it (*Eph. 2:12*). God drove fallen Adam out of the garden and made it impossible for him to return, guarding the entrance with a flaming sword, ready to slay him if he should attempt it. This abundantly shows that he and all in him had lost all right of entering into the family of God. Corrupted, cursed human nature has no right to anything from God.

They are authoritatively transferred from the one family to the other by legal adoption. It is not done in a secret, underhand way, but by authority. 'As many as received him' (that is, Jesus) 'to them he gave the right' (or title by the authority of God's Word) 'to become the children of God' (*John 1:12*).

Investing them with the power, excellence and right to be the sons of God is a legal act. It is called the 'qualifying of us to be partakers of the inheritance of the saints in light' (*Col. 1:12*). It is a judicial exalting of us into membership in that family where God is the Father, Christ the elder brother, all saints and angels brethren and fellow-children, and the inheritance a crown which is immortal and incorruptible that does not fade away.

This authoritative transfer of believers from one family to another is done by the public declaration of the adopted person's being set free from all obligations to the former family to which by nature he was related. This declaration is made to angels, to Satan and to the consciences of believers.

It is declared to angels. They are the sons of God (*Job 1:6; 38:7; Heb. 12:22–24; Rev. 22:9*). So they are part of the family into which the adopted person is to be admitted. Therefore it concerns them to know who are invested with the rights of that family, so that they may discharge their duty to them. To angels, then, it is declared that believers are freed from the family of sin and hell, to become fellow-children and servants with them.

This declaration is made generally by the doctrine of the gospel (*Eph. 3:10*). This wisdom 'that the Gentiles should be fellow-heirs and of the same body as the Jews' is made known to the angels by the church (*Eph. 3:6–10*). The mystery of adopting Gentile sinners, taking them from their slavery in the family of the world in order that they might have the right to be heirs and sons in the family of God, is made known to the angels by the church. It was 'revealed by the Spirit to the prophets and apostles' (*v. 5*).

This declaration is made in part by direct revelation. When any soul in particular is freed from the family of this world, it is revealed to the angels (*Luke 15:10*). Now the angels cannot of themselves know absolutely whether a sinner has truly repented or not. It is revealed to the angels by Christ, when the special care and charge of each repentant sinner is committed to them (*Luke 12:8, 9*). Christ gives the name of his brethren to the angels (*Rev. 3:5*). Christ admits repentant sinners into the family, in which there is an innumerable company of angels (*Heb. 12:22*). Then Christ declares to the angels that these repentant sinners are now sons. So now the angels are able to carry out their duty to them (*Heb. 1:14*).

It is declared to Satan as the one who has been judged and condemned. When the Lord Christ delivers a soul from the power of that strong, armed one, he binds him, so that he can no longer exercise that power and dominion over the soul. So by this means, Satan knows that such a person has been set free from his family and that all his future attempts to try and get that soul back are doomed to failure, for that soul is now the possession and inheritance of the Lord Christ.

It is declared to the conscience of the adopted person. The Spirit of Christ testifies to the heart and conscience of a believer that he is freed from all obligations to the family of Satan and has now become a son of God (Rom. 8:14, 15). The Spirit of Christ enables him to cry 'Abba, Father' (*Gal. 4:6*).

There is an authoritative ingrafting of the believer actually into the family of God and the admitting of him into the whole right and title of sonship

The believer is given a new name in a white stone (*Rev. 2:17*). Believers change their names, which they had in their old family, to take the name of the family into which they are legally adopted. This new name is 'a child of God'. That is the new name given in adoption, and no-one knows what is in that name, but only he that receives it. And this new name is given and written on a white stone, which is the certificate of admission into the house of God. It is the white stone of judicial acquittal. Our adoption by the Spirit rests on our absolution in the blood of Jesus. Therefore the new name in the white stone is the privilege based on the discharge from all obligations to the old family. The new name gives the right and title to the new family.

The believer's name is enrolled in the catalogue of the household of God, admitting him into its fellowship. This is called the 'writing of the house of Israel' (*Ezek. 13:9*). This is the roll in which all the names of Israel, the family of God, are written. God has a catalogue of his household. Christ knows his sheep by name. When God writes up the people, he declares that 'this man was born in Zion' (*Psa. 87:6*). This is an extract from the Lamb's book of life.

The believer's acceptance with God is testified to his conscience, enabling him to behave as a child of God should behave (*Rom. 8:15; Gal. 4:5, 6*).

The last two things required for adoption are that the adopted person is freed from all obligations to the family from which he has been taken and is admitted into all the rights and privileges of the family into which he has been adopted. Now, because these two things are the issues of adoption in which saints have communion with Christ, I shall deal with them together.

We need to know what we receive when we are adopted.

WHEN WE ARE ADOPTED, WE FIRST OF ALL RECEIVE LIBERTY

The Spirit of the Lord that was upon the Lord Jesus anointed him to proclaim liberty to the captives (*Isa. 61:1*). And 'where the Spirit of the Lord is,' (that is, the Spirit of Christ given to us by him because we are sons) 'there is liberty' (*II Cor. 3:17*). All spiritual liberty is from the Spirit of adoption. And all that pretends to be spiritual liberty is nothing but licentiousness. This is what Paul says (*Gal. 4:6, 7*).

The believer is set free from all obligations to the family from which he has been taken. Believers are freed from the instituted law of ordinances which, on the testimony of the apostles, was a burden which neither they nor their fathers in the faith could bear (*Acts 15:10*). So Christ 'blotted out this handwriting of ordinances that was against them, and took it out of the way, nailing it to the cross' (*Col. 2:14*). And Paul, after a long argument concerning the freedom we have from the law, ends with this injunction, 'Stand fast in the liberty by which Christ has made us free' (*Gal. 5:1*).

In what way believers are freed from the moral law

Believers are freed from the terror of the moral law (*Heb. 12:18–22*). The moral law was given in such a way that it caused the people to fear and tremble. They were frightened into obedience. It is from this that we are freed. We are not called to obey from fear and terror.

Believers are freed from the moral law as the means of making them righteous and so acceptable to God. Because of sin, no-one could perfectly obey the law and so be justified (*Rom. 8:2, 3; Gal. 3:21–33*). It is by the righteousness of Christ that we are freed from justifying ourselves by perfect obedience to the moral law (*Rom. 8:3*).

Believers are freed from the judgement, curse and condemnation of the moral law (*Gal. 3:13; Heb. 2:14, 15*). Some pretend to be freed by Christ when they have only been freed from man-made rules and regulations (*Col. 2:20–22*). To these we were never in bondage.

There is also a freedom in the family of God as well as freedom from the family of Satan. Sons are free. Their obedience is free obedience. They have the Spirit of the Lord and where he is, there is freedom (*II Cor. 3:17*). As the Spirit of adoption, he is opposed to the spirit of bondage (*Rom. 8:15*). Now this freedom of our Father's family which we have as sons and children, being adopted by Christ through the Spirit, is a spiritual largeness of heart by which the children of God freely, willingly, genuinely without fear, terror, bondage or constraint, set out in Christ to live a life of holy obedience. This is our liberty in our Father's family.

There are Gibeonites outwardly attending the family of God that do the service of his house. This is the drudgery of their lives. The motive which drives them to obey is a spirit of bondage leading to fear (*Rom. 8:15*). The rule of their obedience is the law robed in all its terror, exacting perfect obedience without mercy. The reason why they do it is because they desire to flee from the wrath to come, to question conscience, and because they seek to make themselves righteous. So in this servile, painful, fruitless way, they seek to serve all their days.

But the saints, being adopted, freely and willingly obey out of the fulness and gratitude of their hearts. David says, 'I will walk at liberty, for I seek your precepts' (*Psa. 119:45; Isa. 61.1; Luke 4:18; Rom. 8:2, 21; Gal. 4:7; 5:1, 13; James 1:25; John 8:32, 33, 36; Rom. 6:18; I Pet. 2:16*). Now this son-like freedom of the Spirit leading to obedience lies in many things.

Son-like obedience lies in life and love. Life gives power to obey. Love gives joy to obedience. It is the law of the Spirit of life in Christ Jesus that sets us free from the law of sin and death (*Rom. 8:2*). The Spirit of life in Christ Jesus enables them to freely and willingly obey. They 'walk after the Spirit' (*v. 1*). Paul said, 'Christ lives in me, and the life which I now live in the flesh, I live by the faith of the Son of God' (*Gal. 2:20*). The life which Paul lived in the flesh was the life of obedience to God, which he was enabled to live by Christ living in him. There is, then, power for us all to live a life of obedience to God when Christ dwells in us. The Spirit of life from Christ enables us to obey.

The difference between the liberty of slaves and that of children

Slaves find freedom when released from their duties. Children find their freedom in doing their duty. There is no greater mistake in the world than the idea that the freedom of sons in God's house lies in choosing whether they will obey or not, whether they will serve or not, whether they will do their duty or not. This is a freedom stolen by slaves, not a liberty given by the Spirit to sons.

The liberty of sons is in the inward spiritual freedom of their hearts gladly and willingly obeying God in everything.

Love gives joy and delight in obedience. 'If you love me,' says Christ, 'keep my commandments' (*John 14:15*). 'Love,' says Paul, 'is the fulfilling of the law' (*Rom. 13:10*).

Jacob's hard service was not burdensome to him, because of his love for Rachel. In the same way, no duty is burdensome or grievous to a saint, because of his love for Christ. 'There is no fear in love; but perfect love casts out fear' (*I John 4:18*).

When a person obeys out of love, then fear is cast out. Fear arises when our obedience is to be judged and may be condemned. So where there is life and love, there is freedom and a willing obedience.

The one whom they obey is the one whom they love and desire above all things. To unrepentant sinners, God is terrible. But to his adopted ones, he is altogether lovely. To believers, God is seen as a Father. They call him Father, not merely in word, but in the spirit of sons (*Gal. 4:6*). They do not, like others, see God as a hard taskmaster, but they go to him as one who lives and loves them. Receiving love from the Father, they pour out their love on him.

Their obedience is motivated by love (*II Cor. 5:14*).

Their obedience is from a willing heart (*Rom. 6:13; 12:1*).

Their obedience is ruled by the law of liberty. The law of liberty is the law stripped of its terrifying, killing, condemning, cursing power, and made by the blood of Jesus, pleasant, lovely and helpful.

THE SECOND THING THE CHILDREN OF GOD HAVE BY ADOPTION IS A TITLE OR PRIVILEGE

The children of God have the right and title to all the privileges of the family into which they are adopted. The reason which Sarah gave for the expulsion of Ishmael was that he was the son of the bondwoman and so no genuine child of the family (*Gen. 21:10*). Therefore, he could have no right to share the inheritance with Isaac. Paul's argument is, 'We are no more servants but sons; and if sons, then heirs' (*Rom. 8:14–17*). Therefore, we have a right and title to all the privileges of sons. And not being born to this, for we were by nature children of wrath, we have this right by adoption.

Believers have a right and title to all the privileges of Christ's ministry here on earth. God has given Jesus Christ to be the 'head over all things to the church, which is his body' (*Eph. 1:22, 23*). God has set up Christ to minister all spiritual things to God's family on earth. His ministry is for the benefit and good of the many sons whom he intends to bring to glory (*Heb. 2:10; Eph. 4:8–13*). The whole aim of the Lord Jesus' ministry is 'for the perfecting of the saints for the work of ministry'. All is for them. All is for the family. In this ministry, the faithfulness of Christ is experienced. He is faithful in all the house of God (*Heb. 3:2; I Cor. 3:22, 23*).

It is true that the Word is preached to all the world, to gather in God's elect, who are scattered about the world, and to leave the rest without excuse. But the chief reason the Lord Christ had in setting up a preaching ministry is to gather in those heirs of salvation to the enjoyment of that feast of fat things which he has prepared for them in his house.

The church is the 'house of God' (*I Tim 3:15; Heb. 3:6*). In the church, Christ keeps and maintains his whole family, ruling them according to his mind and will. Now who shall have any right in the house of God except his own children? We will not allow a right to any but our own children in our houses. Will God then allow any right in his house to any but his children? Is it right to 'take the children's bread and cast it to dogs'? We shall see that none but children have any right or title to the privileges and advantages of the house of God if we consider the following two things.

Consider the nature of God's house. It is made up of 'living stones' (*I Pet. 2:5*). All those in this house are a 'chosen generation, a royal priesthood, a holy nation, his own special people' (*I Pet. 2:9*). They are 'saints and faithful brethren' (*Col. 1:2*). Every one of them is righteous (*Isa. 60:21*). The whole fabric of the house is glorious (*Isa. 54:11–14*). The way of the house is 'a way of holiness', in which the unclean shall not walk (*Isa. 35:8*). In this house are the 'sons and daughters of the Lord Almighty' (*II Cor. 6:17, 18*). All others are excluded (*Rev. 21:27*). It is true that often other persons creep into the great house of God. So in this house there are not only 'vessels of gold and silver, but also of wood and earth' (*II Tim. 2:20*). But they only creep in, they have no right nor title to it (*Jude 4*). It is clear, therefore, that none but God's adopted children have a right to any place in this house.

Consider the privileges of that house. These privileges will not suit any others but the children of God. Is food given to a dead man? Will he grow strong by it? Will he thrive on it? The things of the family and house of God are food for living souls, and only God's children are alive. All others are dead in trespasses and sins. Look at any of the things which saints enjoy in the family of God and you will find that not one of them are suited to unbelievers. To give to unbelievers the things enjoyed by saints would be to 'cast pearls before swine'.

Only the children of God have the right and title to the things of God. They have fellowship with one another and with the Father and his Son Jesus Christ. They set forth the Lord's death till he comes again. They are entrusted with all the ordinances of God's house. And who shall deny them the enjoyment of this right, or keep them from what Christ has bought for them? And the Lord will give them hearts to make use of this privilege and not to wander on the mountains, forgetting their resting place.

They have a right and title to the future fulness of the inheritance that is purchased for this whole family by Jesus Christ (*Rom. 8:17; Heb. 12:23*). As 'firstborn, they are heirs'. So the whole weight of glory that is prepared for them is called the inheritance (*Col. 1:12*). They are heirs of all that was promised to Abraham in and with Christ (*Gal. 3:29*).

THE THREE-FOLD INHERITANCE OF THE CHILDREN OF GOD

The children of God are heirs to the promise (Gal. 3:29; Heb. 6:17). God shows to 'the heirs of the promise, the immutability of his counsel'. Abraham, Isaac and Jacob are said to be 'heirs of the same promise' (*Heb. 11:9*). God had, from the foundation of the world, made a most excellent promise in Christ containing a deliverance from all evil and an obligation to pour out all good things on them. The promise contains a deliverance from all the evil which the guilt of sin and dominion of Satan had brought upon them and investing them with all spiritual blessing in heavenly places in Christ Jesus. So the Holy Spirit calls it a 'promise of the eternal inheritance' (*Heb. 9:15*). This is what the adopted children of God are heirs to.

The children of God are heirs of righteousness (*Heb. 11:7*). Noah was an heir of the righteousness which is by faith, which Peter calls being 'heirs of the grace of life' (*I Pet. 3:7*). James puts both these together (*James 2:5*). Paul tells us that 'we have obtained an inheritance', which he also places with the righteousness of faith (*Acts 26:18*). Now, by this righteousness, grace and inheritance, is not only meant that righteousness which we are actually made partakers of here on earth, but also the perfection of that righteousness in glory.

The children of God are 'heirs of salvation' and 'heirs according to the hope of eternal life' (*Heb. 1:14; Titus 3:7*). Peter calls this an 'incorruptible inheritance' (*I Pet. 1:4*). Paul calls it the 'reward of the inheritance' (*Col. 3:24*). The 'reward of the inheritance' is all that light and holiness which they already enjoy.

The foundation of the full salvation by Christ is the promises. The means to this full salvation are righteousness and salvation. The fulness of that salvation is eternal glory. To all these the sons of God have a right and title. They are made heirs with Christ. He is their portion and inheritance and they are his portion and inheritance.

Saints also have a right and title to the things of this world and to all the things that God is pleased to entrust to them

Christ is the 'heir of all things' (*Heb. 1:2*). All right and title to the things of creation was lost and forfeited by sin. The Lord, by his sovereign will, had given all things on earth for man's use. But when sin entered, all creation ceased to be subject to man, and instead of revealing the glory of God, became subject to meaninglessness and the curse. They no longer show forth the glory of God to man. Man, having lost dominion over all things on earth, has no right or title or claim to them. But God, intending to save a part of mankind, does not immediately destroy the works of creation, but keeps them for the use of his saints. So the right and title of dominion over all things in this world is given to them in Christ, the second Adam. God appoints Christ 'heir of all things'. So his adopted ones, being 'fellow-heirs with Christ', also have a right and title to creation. But the following things need to be noted.

The right that believers have is not the same right that Christ has. Christ has the sovereign and supreme right to do what he will with his own. The right that believers have is subordinate to Christ. They are accountable for the use of those things to which they have a right and title. The right of Christ is the right of the Lord of the house. The right of the saints is the right of servants of the house.

That all the children of God have a right to the whole earth, which is the Lord's, is seen in the following two instances.

He who is the sovereign Lord of creation keeps it for one reason only. He keeps it for the use of his saints.

Christ has promised to give them the kingdom and the dominion of it. He governs this earth and all creation so that 'all things work together for the good of his saints'.

This right is a spiritual right. It does not give them the civil right to possess all things for themselves. God has providentially arranged the civil bounds of the inheritances of men (*Acts 17:26*). So no one particular adopted person has any right to any portion of earthly things to which they have no civil right or title.

Whatever God is pleased to give his saints, they have a right to, but only through Christ, who has redeemed it from the curse that came upon all creation because of sin. So they are led to use the things of the world for holy purposes, because what the Father in his providence gives them are seen as pledges of his love, washed in the blood of Christ and motives to live to his praise who gives them all things richly to enjoy.

Unbelievers may have a civil right to many things of earth. But they do not have a spiritual, sanctified right to a place in the house of God or to any of the privileges of that house. Unbelievers do not use anything they have for the glory of God and have kept them from the children of God for whose sakes they (that is, unbelievers) are kept from destruction. What judgment awaits them! God will say, 'I have allowed you to enjoy many things in this world. What have you laid out for the spread of the gospel? What have you given to the poor, especially the poor saints? Have you been willing to lay down all for my sake?'

And they will answer, 'Lord, we did indeed possess many things in this world. But we treated these things as our own to do with as we pleased. We have done nothing for the gospel, nor for the poor, nor for your saints. We have spent it on ourselves.'

Then the Lord will say, 'And what right and title have you to these things? I have restored these things, lost by sin, to give to my saints and to them alone. Why have you stolen that which is not yours? Give me back what is mine.' Then the wicked will be sent away naked and ashamed from God's presence. What, then, will men do?

OTHER PRIVILEGES OF OUR ADOPTION

Boldness with God by Christ (*Heb. 10:19*). Affliction coming from love and leading to our spiritual good (*Heb. 12:3–6*). The privilege of being called sons of God (*I John 3:1*). Being heirs and joint-heirs with Christ (*Rom. 8:17*). Being predestinated to be conformed to the image of God's Son (*Rom. 8:29*). Being called Christ's brethren (*Heb. 2:11*). Fellowship in Christ's sufferings (*Rom. 8:17*). He learned obedience by what he suffered, and every son that he receives is to be disciplined (*Heb. 12:6*). Fellowship in his kingdom (*II Tim. 2:12*). We shall reign with him.

18: *The Foundation of our Communion with the Holy Spirit*

The foundation of all our communion with the Holy Spirit lies in his being sent by Jesus Christ to be our Comforter or helper.

JOHN 16:1–7

When Jesus Christ was about to leave the world, among other things, he warned his disciples of the sort of reception they would receive from the world. He does not want them to be put off or offended by the persecution they are about to face (*v. 1*). He warns them that they will be excommunicated, both by the ecclesiastical and also by the civil powers. These powers would even think they were serving God by persecuting and killing them (*v. 2*). These worldly powers will be set against them because they are spiritually blind and desperately ignorant (*v. 3*).

Jesus tells them these things, not to frighten them in their time of grief and sorrow, but that they might remember that he had warned them and so be encouraged in their trials by his deity and omniscience (*v. 4*). He did not warn them before of these things because he was then with them. But now he was about to leave them. The disciples were so filled with grief and sorrow that they did not even ask him where he was going. If they knew that he was going to take possession of his glory and to carry out the work of their salvation, their hearts would not be so filled with sorrow and fears (*vv. 5, 6*). And so he ends with the declaration, 'Nevertheless, I tell you the truth. It is to your advantage that I go away; for if I do not go away, the helper will not come to you; but if I depart, I will send him to you' (*v. 7*).

So the Lord Christ would have us know this great truth, that the presence of the Holy Spirit with believers as Comforter and helper, sent by him as promised, is better and more profitable to believers than his bodily presence can ever be, now that he has made the one sacrifice for sin which he came into the world to offer.

The Holy Spirit is promised to the elect as the Spirit of sanctification, to convert them and make them believers. The Holy Spirit is also promised as the Spirit of comfort and help to believers, to give them the privileges of the death and purchase of Christ. It is as the Spirit of comfort and help that he is spoken of here.

If we ask, 'Where does the Holy Spirit come from?' we are told that he 'proceeds from the Father' (*John 15:26*). As the Spirit of the Father and the Son, proceeding from both eternally, he receives his substance and personality. This great truth is to be received by faith, and I do not intend to deal with it now.

But the Spirit's 'proceeding' in respect of the work of grace he comes to do is what we must look at now. The 'proceeding of the Spirit' refers to his being sent by Christ after his ascension. 'I will send him who proceeds from the Father.' As God is said to 'come out of his place' (*Isa. 26:21*), not by any change in him, but because of the new work he has come to do, so it follows that the Lord comes out of his place 'to punish the inhabitants of the earth'. But it is for his special work of testifying to Christ that he is said to 'proceed'. This cannot be said of him in respect to his eternal procession, but of his actual work in the purpose of salvation. So also, for this same purpose, it is said of Christ, 'He came forth from God'. The single mention of the Father in this place, and not of the Son, is due to the special office of each person in the Trinity in the working out of the plan of salvation, the mystery of which Christ reveals to his disciples. But Christ also sends the Holy Spirit to us (*John 16:7*).

COMMUNION WITH THE HOLY SPIRIT

We have communion with the Holy Spirit in his willingness to be the Comforter and helper. The Spirit willingly proceeds from the Father and the Son in this work of salvation. He is as willing to take upon himself the work of comforter and helper as the Son was willing to take on himself the work of redeemer.

The order of persons in the work of salvation is, firstly, the Father and his loving purpose to send the Spirit. Then we have the asking of the Son, which is followed by the willing proceeding of the Holy Spirit.

This testifies to our special communion with the Father in love, the Son in grace, and the Holy Spirit in his work as comforter and helper. This is the way into fellowship with the Holy Spirit to which we are called. His gracious and blessed will, his infinite and wonderful willingness to come down to us, all the works he enables us to do and all the privileges he brings to us, of which we are made partakers, is what our souls by faith receive from him. And our response is to pour out on him all our gratitude and thankfulness. This, then, is the first great thing in our communion with the Holy Spirit.

We have communion with the Holy Spirit in the way he comes to us from the Father

The Holy Spirit is freely given to us by the Father. We do not have to buy him. 'The Father,' says Jesus, 'shall give you another helper' (*John 14:16*). Jesus also said, 'How much more will your Father give the Holy Spirit to those who ask him'. That which is a gift is free. The fruit of grace is given by grace. So the Spirit is said to be received by the gospel, not by the law (*Gal. 3:2*). We receive the Spirit by grace alone and not by making ourselves worthy to receive him. All the Spirit's workings are called 'charismata' or 'free gifts'. He is freely given and he works freely, looking for no payment from us. So we receive him as a free gift. This is how the Spirit is to be seen, to be asked for and to be received, as a free gift. This is what faith takes hold of in our communion with the Holy Spirit. So the soul rejoices in the comforter for two reasons. Firstly, because he is willing to come to us and, secondly, because he is willing to be given to us.

The Holy Spirit is sent to us by the authority of the Father and of the Son (*John 14:26; 15:26; 16:7*). This shows the willingness of the Holy Spirit to be under authority, when he is equal with the Father and the Son in the Godhead. It is the office of the Holy Spirit to be an advocate for us and a help to us, and it is for the fulfilment of this work that he is authoritatively sent by the Father and the Son. On this authoritative sending of the Spirit rests the right understanding of many mysteries of the gospel and our fellowship with him.

THE SIN AGAINST THE HOLY SPIRIT

From this arises the sin against the Holy Spirit and why it is unpardonable. No other sin is considered to be as rebellious as is the sin of rejecting the Holy Spirit. It is considered to be the height of rebellion to reject the Holy Spirit, because he comes in the name and authority of the Father and the Son from whom and by whom he is sent. Therefore, to sin against him is to sin against the whole authority of God, all the love of the Trinity and all the utmost willingness of each person of the Godhead to take the place and office appointed him for our salvation. To reject the Spirit is to reject the love of the Triune God, Father, Son and Holy Spirit.

We are to pray to the Father and to the Son for the Spirit as sent by them (Luke 11:13). The Holy Spirit, being God, is no less to be prayed to and called on than the Father and the Son. When we pray to the Spirit, we remember that he is God over all, blessed for ever. But when we pray for him from the Father and the Son, we pray for him as sent by the Father and the Son to complete the work of salvation in us.

As sent by the Father and the Son, we are not to grieve him (*Eph. 4:30*). We are not to grieve him because he comes to us in the name and with the love and willingness of the whole Trinity to bring us to eternal salvation. So he expects to be received cheerfully and not to be shown the door!

As sent by the Father and the Son, the Holy Spirit is said to be poured out or shed on us (*Titus 3:6*). This was the way the giving of the Holy Spirit was expressed in the Old Testament. The mystery of his being sent by the Father and the Son was not then clearly revealed. The expression 'poured out' refers to the calling of the gentiles and the rejection of the Jews (*Isa. 32:15; 44:3; Zech. 12:10*). The Holy Spirit in the Old Testament was pictured as coming like water or rain. Water is needed and is effective for life and growth and there is plenty of it in the world.

So the giving, sending and pouring out of the Spirit gives us three great properties of the covenant of grace:

(1) It is free: the Holy Spirit is given. (2) It is ordered in all things and sure: he comes from the love of the Father and the purchase of the blood of the Son. (3) It is effective: the Holy Spirit is poured out.

THE HOLY SPIRIT IS RECEIVED BY BELIEVERS

Our receiving the Holy Spirit as the Spirit of sanctification is

[172]

a mere passive reception, as an empty cup receives water. He comes like the wind on the dead bones (*Ezek. 37*). He comes to dead hearts and brings them to life by an act of almighty power. But as the helper or comforter, he comes as one received and welcomed. In this sense, our Saviour tells us that 'the world cannot receive him' (*John 14:17*). None can receive the Spirit as the comforter or helper who has not first been brought from death to life by the Spirit of sanctification. As the comforter, believers can receive the Spirit, because they know him. Here, then, is an active receiving of the Spirit. He is received by the power of faith (*Gal. 3:2*). The preaching of the gospel gives birth to faith in them, enabling them to receive the Spirit. So 'believing' is put as the qualification for our receiving the Holy Spirit (*John 7:39*). Therefore, it is only believers who receive the Holy Spirit, and they receive him by faith.

There are three special acts of faith by which we receive the Spirit:

(1) Faith receives the Spirit as the Spirit promised in the covenant of grace. Faith takes hold of the promises (*Heb. 4:2*). And we receive the promise of the Spirit by faith (*Gal. 3:14*). So the receiving of the Spirit through faith is receiving him as promised. Faith sees the promise of God and of Jesus Christ sending the Spirit to meet all the needs and to satisfy all the desires of believers.

(2) Faith receives the Spirit by prayer. He is given as the Spirit of prayer in order that we may ask for him as the comforter (*Luke 11:13*). Praying for the Holy Spirit is the most important work faith has to do in this world.

(3) Faith receives the Spirit by being alert to him and his secret work in our hearts. Faith looks on the Spirit as he is purchased by Christ and promised by the Father. Therefore faith seeks him from God and so receives him.

THE HOLY SPIRIT ABIDES WITH BELIEVERS

The Holy Spirit indwells every believer as the Spirit of sanctification (*Rom. 8:11*). He lives in us as his temple (*I Cor. 6:19*). Jesus said, 'He shall abide with you for ever' (*John 14:16*). Now all the difficulty in this promise lies in the fact that, whereas the Spirit of sanctification dwells in us always and therefore it is impossible for us to utterly lose our holiness, the Spirit as comforter and helper does not seem to abide with us always. So how is it that the Comforter does not seem to abide with us always, when he abides with us for ever as the Spirit of sanctification?

The Holy Spirit is promised to us to abide with us for ever in contrast to the abiding of Christ. Christ in the flesh had been with his disciples for a little while and now was leaving them and returning to the Father. Christ had been their comforter for a little while. Now he promised them another comforter. But they were afraid that he would only be with them for a little while as well. Then their condition would be worse than ever. But Christ tells them not to worry. This was the last dispensation. When he had gone, the comforter was to do all the work that remained to be done. There is no further comforter to be looked for. The comforter who would come to them would never depart from them but would always abide with them.

The comforter may always abide with us, though not always comfort us. He comforts according to his sovereign will. As the Spirit of holiness, he must make us holy, because the temple of God is holy. But he does not always have to comfort us.

The Comforter often brings comfort to us when we do not receive it. The oasis is near, though we do not always see it. We often refuse to be comforted. The Spirit as sanctifier comes with power to conquer an unbelieving heart. The

Spirit as Comforter comes with help and encouragement to be received by a believing heart. He often speaks, but we do not always believe that it is his voice. 'In the day of my trouble,' said David, 'I sought the Lord; my hand was stretched out in the night without ceasing; my soul refused to be comforted' (*Psa. 77:2*).

The Comforter actually never leaves the believing soul with no comfort at all. A man may be in the dark, under a cloud, refusing comfort and actually finding none and feeling none. But the Spirit is the source of all comfort and in due time his comfort will be felt. God promises that he will heal sinners and restore comfort to them (*Isa. 57:8*).

The Comforter, being sent and given, abides with the souls of believers and does not leave them. He reveals himself in various ways and by various works.

He works effectively (*I Cor. 12:11*). All that the Holy Spirit purposes to work in us, he fully accomplishes by his almighty power. So all that we have from the Holy Spirit is by his power working effectively in us.

He works sovereignly. The Holy Spirit distributes to everyone as he wills (*I Cor. 12:11*). He gives one gift to one person and another to another person. This he does of his own freedom of will, ruled by his own judgment and choice. So the saints are kept in constant dependence on him and his sovereignty. If the Holy Spirit gives to us as he wills, then we should be content with that which he gives us.

He works freely (*Acts 2:4*). He worked in the disciples the ability to speak in other tongues and he did this freely. So in the work of our salvation, the freedom and liberty of each of the persons of the Godhead is respected. The love of the Father in sending the Son is free and his sending the Son in no way prejudices the freedom and love of the Son in laying down his life for us. So also the satisfaction and purchase made by the Son in no way prejudices the freedom of the

Father's grace in pardoning and accepting us on account of what the Son has done.

So the sending of the Spirit by the Father and the Son does not take away the freedom of the Spirit's will in doing his work in us. What the Spirit gives he gives freely and the reason for this is that the will of the Father, Son and Holy Spirit is essentially the same, so that when one person of the Godhead acts, he acts according to the will and purpose of all.

It is the same with the Holy Spirit's workings in us, of which power, choice and freedom are the marks.

19: *The Things in which we have Communion with the Holy Spirit*

THE FIRST GENERAL WORK OF THE HOLY SPIRIT IS TO BRING TO
MIND THE WORDS AND PROMISES OF CHRIST

The first thing in which we have communion with the Holy Spirit is his work of bringing to mind the things that Jesus said (*John 14:26*). There are two promises in this verse. There is the promise of the Spirit's teaching, which I will deal with under his work of anointing believers, and there is the promise of 'bringing to remembrance all things that Jesus said'.

The work of bringing to remembrance things that Jesus said is the first general promise concerning the Spirit's work as comforter.

This promise first concerned the apostles. Christ promised his apostles that the Holy Spirit would bring back to their minds, by a direct work of almighty power, the things that he had said to them, so that by his inspiration they might be enabled to write and preach them for the good and benefit of his church (*II Pet. 1:21*). The apostles had forgotten much of what Christ had said to them, or might possibly do so. And what they did remember by their natural ability was not a sufficient foundation for them to write an infallible rule of faith for the church. It would be by this work of the Spirit that they would be enabled to write such an infallible rule of faith.

This promise of bringing to remembrance all the things that Jesus had spoken is also for the comfort of believers. Christ had been speaking to his disciples to comfort them by giving them precious promises of his help and strength in this life. He told them of the love of the Father, of the glory he was providing for them, which was full of unspeakable joy. 'But,' Christ says, 'I know how unable you are to make use of these things for your own comfort. The Spirit, therefore, will bring them back to your minds in their full strength, so that you will find that comfort in them which I intended.' And this is one reason why it was necessary for believers that Christ's bodily absence should be more than made up for by the presence of the Spirit. While he was with them, what little effect his promises had on their hearts! But when the Spirit came, how full of joy did he make all things to them. He brings the promises of Christ to our minds and hearts to comfort us, to bring us the joy of them and that far beyond the joy the disciples found in them when Christ spoke to them on earth. The gracious influences of the promises were then restrained so that the dispensation of the Spirit might be seen to be more glorious than that of the giving of the law.

Christ told the disciples that the effect of the Holy Spirit's work in bringing things to their remembrance would be peace (*John 14:27*). They would be freed from worried, anxious minds and fearful hearts. It is stupid to rely on our natural abilities to remember the promises of Christ. But when the Comforter undertakes the work, then all is well. Our Saviour Christ, then, left to his Spirit the powerful effect of his promises which he personally gave his apostles in their great distress. We may therefore see where all the spiritual comfort we have in this world comes from, and so we may have fellowship with the Holy Spirit in this his work.

The Holy Spirit does his work powerfully. A believer may be in the saddest and darkest condition imaginable. Even so, the Holy Spirit is able to break through all this and bring to mind the promises of Christ. By this work, the Holy Spirit enables Christians to sit in dungeons, rejoice in flames and glory in troubles. If he brings to mind the promises of Christ for our comfort, neither Satan nor man, neither sin nor the world, nor even death itself shall take away our comfort. Saints who have communion with the Holy Spirit know this only too well. Sometimes the heavens are black over them, and the earth trembles under them. Disasters and distresses appear which are so full of horror and darkness that they are tempted to give up in despair. So how greatly are their spirits revived when the Holy Spirit brings the words of Christ to their minds for their comfort and joy. Thus, believers are not dependent on outward circumstances for their happiness, for they have the inward and powerfully effective work of the Holy Spirit, to whom they give themselves up by faith.

The Holy Spirit does his work sovereignly. The Holy Spirit distributes to everyone as he wills. So the believer may at one time be full of joy and, at another, full of distress. Every promise at one time brings great joy when troubles are great and heavy; yet at another time, when only suffering a little, he finds no joy in the promises, however much he seeks for it. The reason is simple. The Holy Spirit distributes as he wills. So there are no rules or course of procedure given to us to follow in order to get peace and joy in the promises. In this way, faith learns to wait on the sovereign will and pleasure of the Holy Spirit.

The Holy Spirit works freely and without payment. Because much of the comfort which comes by the promises depends on the sovereign will of the Holy Spirit, so we find that comfort comes unexpectedly when the heart has every reason in the world to expect distress and sorrow. This is often the first means of restoring a backsliding soul who might justly be expecting to be utterly cast off.

The life and soul of all our comforts are treasured up in the promises of Christ. They are the breasts from which we suck the milk of godly comfort. Who does not know how powerless these promises are in the bare letter, even though we may meditate long on them, as well as how unexpectedly they burst in on the soul, bringing great comfort and joy. Faith deals especially with the Holy Spirit. Faith considers the promises themselves, looks up to the Spirit and waits for the Spirit to bring life and comfort into them. No sooner does the soul begin to feel the life of a promise warming his heart, freeing him from fear, worries and troubles, than it may know, and it ought to know, that the Holy Spirit is doing his work. This will add to the believer's joy and lead him into deeper fellowship with the Holy Spirit.

THE SECOND GENERAL WORK OF THE HOLY SPIRIT IS TO GLORIFY CHRIST (*John 16:14*)

If the work of the Spirit is to glorify Christ, then we may see what sort of a spirit that is who sets himself up in the place of Christ, calling himself 'the vicar of Christ' or 'another Christ'. The work of the Comforter is to glorify Christ. So any spirit that claims to be of Christ and does not seek to glorify that Christ who spoke to his apostles is clearly a false spirit.

But how will the Comforter glorify Christ? 'He,' says Christ, 'shall take of mine.' What these things are is told us in the next verse. 'All things that the Father has are mine, therefore I said he shall take of mine.' Christ is not speaking of the essence and essential properties of the Father and the Son, but he is speaking of the grace which is brought to us by the Father and the Son. This is what Christ calls 'my things', because they are the 'things' purchased by his mediation. They are also the 'things of the Father', because in his eternal love, he has provided them to be brought to us by the blood of his Son. They are the fruits of his election. 'These,' said Christ, 'the Comforter shall receive. They shall be committed to him so that he may bring them to you for your good and for your comfort in trouble. So he shall show, declare and make them known to you.' As Comforter, he reveals to the souls of sinners the good things of the covenant of grace, which the Father has provided and the Son has purchased. He shows to us mercy, grace, forgiveness, righteousness and acceptance with God. It is vital to know that these are the things of Christ which he has procured for us. They are shown to us for our comfort and establishment. These things the Holy Spirit effectively conveys to the souls of believers, and makes them known to them for their own good; that they were originally from the Father, prepared from eternity in his love and good will; that they were purchased for them by Christ and laid up for them in the covenant of grace for their use. In this way, Christ is magnified and glorified in their hearts and they then fully realise what a glorious Saviour and Redeemer he is. It is by the work of the Holy Spirit that a believer glorifies and honours Christ for the eternal redemption he has purchased for him. 'No-one can say that Jesus is Lord, but by the Holy Spirit' (*I Cor. 12:3*).

THE THIRD GENERAL WORK OF THE HOLY SPIRIT IS TO 'POUR THE LOVE OF GOD INTO OUR HEARTS' (*Rom. 5:5*)

That it is the love of God to us and not our love to God which is here meant is clear from the context. The love of God is either the love of his purpose to do us good or the love of acceptance and approval by him. Both these are called the love of God in Scripture. Now, how can these be poured into our hearts? This can be done only by giving us a spiritual understanding of them. God pours the Holy Spirit abundantly on us and he pours out the love of God into our hearts. That is, the Holy Spirit so persuades us that God loves us that our souls are filled with joy and comfort. This is his work and he does it effectively. To persuade a poor, sinful soul that God in Jesus Christ loves him, delights in him, is well pleased with him and only has thoughts of kindness towards him is an inexpressible mercy.

This is the special work of the Holy Spirit and by this special work we have communion with the Father in his love, which is poured into our hearts. So not only do we rejoice in and glorify the Holy Spirit who does this work, but in the Father also, whose love it is. It is the same in respect of the Son, in taking the things of Christ and showing them to us. What we have of heaven in this world lies in this work of the Holy Spirit.

THE FOURTH GENERAL WORK OF THE HOLY SPIRIT IS TO BEAR WITNESS WITH OUR SPIRITS THAT WE ARE THE CHILDREN OF GOD (*Rom. 8:16*)

Sometimes the soul wonders whether it is a child of God or not, because so much of the old nature still remains. So the soul brings out all the evidences to prove its claim to be a true child of God. To support this claim, the Holy Spirit comes and bears witness that the claim is true.

The picture is that of judicial proceedings in a court of law. The judge being seated, the person concerned lays his claim, produces his evidences and pleads his case. Then a person of known and approved integrity comes into the court and testifies on behalf of the claimant. This stops the mouth of all the adversaries and fills the man that pleaded with joy and satisfaction. It is the same with the believer. The soul, by the power of his own conscience, is brought before the law of God. There the soul puts in his plea that he is a true child of God, that he does indeed belong to God's family, and to prove this, he produces all his evidences, everything by which faith gives him a right and title to God. Satan, in the meantime, opposes with all his might. Sin and the law add their opposition also. Many flaws are found in his evidences. The truth of them all is questioned and the soul is left in doubt as to whether he is a child of God or not. Then the Comforter comes and by a word of promise or in some other way, overwhelms the heart with a sure persuasion, putting down all objections, showing that his plea is good and that he is indeed a child of God. And therefore the Holy Spirit is said to 'witness with our spirits that we are children of God.'

At the same time, he enables us to show our love to the Father by acts of obedience to his will, which is called 'crying Abba, Father' (*Gal. 4:6*). But as the Holy Spirit works sovereignly of his own will and pleasure, the believer may be kept in doubt for a long time. The law sometimes seems to prevail, sin and Satan to rejoice and the poor soul is filled with dread about his inheritance. Perhaps by his own witness, from his faith, sanctification and previous experience, he keeps up his claim with some life and comfort. But the work is not done, the conquest is not fully won, until the Spirit, who works freely and effectively, when and how he wills, comes in with his testimony also. Clothing his power with his promise, he makes all parties concerned listen to him and so puts an end to the whole dispute.

In this, he gives us holy fellowship with himself. The soul knows his voice when he speaks. There is something too great in that voice to be only the voice of some created power. When the Lord Jesus Christ at one word stilled the storm, all who were with him knew there was divine power at work (*Matt. 8:25–27*). And when the Holy Spirit with one word stills the storms in the soul, bringing calm and assurance, then the soul knows by experience that divine power is present and so rejoices in that presence.

THE FIFTH GENERAL WORK OF THE HOLY SPIRIT IS HIS WORK IN SEALING US (*Eph. 1:13; 4:30*)

To seal something is to impart the image of the seal to the thing sealed. The character of the seal is stamped on the things sealed. In this sense, the effective communication of the image of God to us should be our sealing. The Spirit in believers, really communicating the image of God in righteousness and true holiness to the soul, seals us. To have the stamp of the Holy Spirit as an evidence to the soul that he has been accepted by God is to be sealed by the Spirit. In this sense, Christ is said to be sealed by God (*John 6:27*). He had impressed on him the power, wisdom and majesty of God.

'Sealing' confirms or ratifies any grant or conveyance made in writing. In such cases, men set their seals to make good and confirm their grants. When this is done, the grants are irrevocable. Sealing also confirms the testimony that is given by anyone of the truth of anything. This is what the Jews did. When anyone had given true witness to any thing or matter and it was received by the judges, they instantly set their seals to it, to confirm it in judgment. So it is said that he who receives the testimony of Christ 'sets to his seal that God is true' (AV) or 'has certified that God is true' (*John 3:33*). The promise is the great grant and conveyance of life and salvation in Christ to the souls of believers. That we may have full assurance of the truth and the irrevocability of the promise, God gives us the Spirit to satisfy our hearts of it. So the Spirit is said to seal us by assuring our hearts of those promises and the faithfulness of the God who promised. But though many expositors take this line, I do not see how this accords with the true meaning of the word. It is not said that the promise is sealed, but that we are sealed. And when we seal a deed or grant to anyone, we do not say the man is sealed, but that the deed or grant is sealed.

Sealing denotes possession and assurance of being kept safe. The object sealed is separated out from unsealed objects. Men set their seals on that which they possess and desire to keep safe for themselves. So quite clearly, in this sense, the servants of God are said to be sealed. They are marked with God's mark as his special ones (*Ezek. 9:4*). So believers are sealed when they are marked for God to be the heirs of the purchased possession and to be kept safe to the day of redemption. Now if this is what is meant, it does not denote the giving of assurance in the heart, but of giving security to the person. The Father gives the elect into the hands of Christ to be redeemed. Christ having redeemed them, in due time they are called by the Spirit and marked for God, and so they give themselves up to the care of the Father.

We are sealed for the day of redemption when, from the stamp, image and character of the Spirit upon our souls, we have a fresh awareness of the love of God given to us, with an assured persuasion of our being accepted by God.

So the Holy Spirit communicates to us his own likeness, which is also the image of the Father and the Son (*II Cor. 3:18*). In this work of his, the Holy Spirit brings us into fellowship with himself. Our likeness to him gives us boldness with him. We look for his works. We pray for his fruits, and when any effect of grace, any awareness of the image of Christ implanted in us persuades and assures us that we are separated and set apart for God, then we have communion with the Holy Spirit in his work of sealing.

THE SIXTH WORK OF THE HOLY SPIRIT IS HIS BEING AN 'EARNEST' OF 'DEPOSIT' OR 'GUARANTEE' (*I Cor. 1:22; 5:5; Eph. 1:13, 14*)

From these verses, we learn that the Spirit himself is the 'earnest, deposit or guarantee'. Each of these words denotes a pledge. A pledge is that property which anyone gives or leaves in the safe keeping of another, to assure him that he will give him, or pay him all that he has promised at some future date. But that which is meant by 'earnest, deposit or guarantee' here is a part of that which is to come. An 'earnest' is part of the price of anything, or part of any grant given beforehand to assure the person to whom it is given that at the appointed time he shall receive the promised whole.

For a thing to be an 'earnest, deposit or guarantee', it must be part of the whole. It must be of the same kind and nature with the whole, just as if we have some money as an 'earnest, deposit or guarantee' that the whole amount will be paid later.

It must be a guarantee of a promise. First, the whole is promised, then the 'earnest' is given as a deposit or guarantee that the promise will be fulfilled. The Holy Spirit is this 'earnest'. God gives us the promise of eternal life. To guarantee this to us, he gives us his Spirit. So the Spirit is the 'earnest, the deposit, the guarantee' of the full inheritance that is promised and purchased.

The Holy Spirit is an 'earnest, deposit and guarantee' on God's part, because God gives him as the best part of the inheritance itself, and because the Holy Spirit is of the same kind and nature as the whole inheritance, as an 'earnest' ought to be. The full inheritance promised is the fulness of the Spirit in the enjoyment of God. When that Spirit which is given to us in this world has perfectly taken away all sin and sorrow and has made us able to enjoy the glory of God in his presence, that is the full inheritance promised. So that the Spirit given to us to make us fit for the enjoyment of God in some measure whilst we are here is the 'earnest or guarantee' of the whole.

God does this to assure us of the inheritance and to guarantee it to us. Having given us his Word, promises, covenant, oath, the revelation of his faithfulness and his immutability as guarantees, all of which exist outside us, he also graciously gives us his Spirit to dwell within us, so that we may have all the security and guarantee of which we are capable (*Isa. 59:21*). What more can be done? He has given us his Holy Spirit. In him we have the first-fruits of glory, the utmost pledge of his love, the earnest or guarantee of the whole.

The Holy Spirit is also the 'earnest, deposit or guarantee' on the part of believers because he gives them an awareness of the love of God for them. The Holy Spirit makes known to believers their acceptance with God, that he is their Father and will deal with them as with children and so, consequently, the inheritance will be theirs. He sends his Spirit into their hearts, 'crying Abba, Father' (*Gal. 4:6*). And what inference do believers draw from this? 'Now we are not servants, but sons, heirs of God and joint-heirs with Christ' (*Gal. 4:7; Rom. 8:17*). So as children of God, we have a right to the inheritance. Of this the Holy Spirit assures us.

The Holy Spirit acquaints believers with their inheritance (*I Cor. 2:9, 10*). As the 'earnest' is the part of the whole, so by the 'earnest' we get a foretaste of the whole. By the Holy Spirit, then, we get a foretaste of the fulness of that glory which God has prepared for those that love him and the more communion we have with the Holy Spirit as an 'earnest', the more we taste of that heavenly glory that awaits us.

THE SEVENTH GENERAL WORK OF THE HOLY SPIRIT IS TO ANOINT BELIEVERS (*II Cor. 1:21; I John 2:20, 27*)

Of the many endowments of Christ which he had from the Spirit with which he was anointed, wisdom, counsel and understanding are the chief things (*Isa. 11:2, 3*). On account of this, all the treasures of wisdom and knowledge are said to be in him (*Col. 2:3*). So the anointing of believers is associated with teaching (*I John. 2:20, 27*). The work of the

[187]

'anointing' is to teach us. The Spirit who anoints us is therefore the Spirit of wisdom, of counsel, of knowledge and understanding in the fear of the Lord. So the great promise of the Comforter was that he should 'teach us' (*John 14:26*). Christ promised that the Comforter would 'guide us into all truth' (*John 16:13*). This teaching us the mind and will of God in the way in which we are taught it by the Spirit our Comforter is the chief part of our anointing by him.

The Spirit teaches by conviction and illumination. So the Spirit teaches the world by the preaching of the Word as promised (*John 16:8*).

The Spirit teaches by sanctification. He opens blind eyes, gives new understanding, shines into our hearts to give us the knowledge of the glory of God in the face of Jesus Christ and enables us to receive spiritual things in a spiritual light (*I Cor. 2:13*). He gives a saving knowledge of the mystery of the gospel. All this is common to believers.

The Spirit teaches by comforting. He makes sweet, useful and joyful to the soul that which he, as the Spirit of sanctification, reveals of the mind and will of God. Here the oil of the Spirit is called the 'oil of gladness', because he brings joy and gladness with his teaching. And the name of Christ is experienced as sweet 'ointment poured forth', that causes souls to run after him with joy and delight (*Song 1:3*). We see it in daily experience that very many have little taste and relish in their souls for these truths which they believe for salvation. But when we are taught by this 'anointing', how sweet is everything we learn of God!

The Spirit teaches us of the love of God in Christ. He makes every gospel truth like well-refined wine to our souls and the good things of the gospel to be a rich feast of good things. He gives us joy and gladness of heart with all that we know of God, which is the great way of keeping the soul close to the truth. By this anointing, the soul is kept from being seduced into error. Truth will readily be exchanged for error when no more sweetness and joy is to be found in it than is to be found in the error. When we find any of the good truths of the gospel coming home to our souls with power, giving us gladness of heart and transforming us into the image and likeness of it, the Holy Spirit is then at his work. He is pouring out his oil.

The Spirit is also the 'Spirit of supplication' (*Zech. 12:10*). It is he who enables us to pray rightly and effectively.

Our prayers may be considered as a spiritual duty required by God. So they are wrought in us by the Spirit of sanctification, who helps us to perform all our duties by exalting all the faculties of the soul.

Our prayers may be considered as a means of keeping up communion with God. The soul is never more lifted up with the love of God than when by the Spirit it is taken into communion with God in prayer. This is the work of the Spirit as comforter.

Here, then, is the wisdom of faith. Faith looks for and meets with the Comforter in all these works of his. Let us not, then, lose their sweetness by remaining in the dark about them, nor fall short of the response required of us in gratitude.

20: *The Holy Spirit and the Hearts of Believers*

THE HOLY SPIRIT COMFORTS AND STRENGTHENS THE HEARTS OF
BELIEVERS (*Acts 9:31*)

This is the chief work of the Holy Spirit in the hearts of
believers. He brings the troubled soul to rest and contentment by getting the believer to think of some spiritually good
thing or actually brings some spiritually good thing to him.
This spiritual good is such that it completely overcomes that
trouble which the soul has been wrestling with. Where
comfort is mentioned, it is always associated with trouble or
suffering (*II Cor. 1:5, 6*).

This comfort is everlasting (*II Thess. 2:16*). It does not
come and go. It abides for ever, because it comes from
everlasting things, such as everlasting love, eternal redemption and an everlasting inheritance.

This comfort is strong (*Heb. 6:18*). As we experience
strong opposition and trouble, so our comfort or consolation
is strong and so unconquerable. It confirms and strengthens
the heart under any evil. It fortifies the soul and makes it able
cheerfully to undergo anything that it is called to undergo.
This comfort is strong because he who brings it is strong.

This comfort is precious. So Paul makes it the great motive
to obedience to which he exhorts the Philippians (*Phil. 2:1*).

The fellowship we have with the Holy Spirit lies, in no
small part, in the comfort or consolation we receive from
him. This teaches us to value his love, to look to him in our
troubles, and to wait on him for his everlasting, strong,
precious comfort.

THE HOLY SPIRIT BRINGS PEACE TO THE HEARTS OF BELIEVERS (*Rom. 15:13*)

The power of the Holy Spirit not only refers to 'hope' but also to our peace in believing. When Christ promised to give the Comforter to his disciples, he also promised to give them his peace (*John 14:26, 27*). Christ gives his peace by giving the Comforter. The peace of Christ lies in the soul's assurance of being accepted by God in personal friendship. So Christ is said to be 'our peace' (*Eph. 2:14*). He slays the enmity between God and us, 'having wiped out the handwriting of requirements that was against us' (*Col. 2:14*). Being assured of our justification and acceptance with God in Christ is the foundation of our peace (*Rom. 5:1*). To know that we are delivered from eternal wrath, from being hated, cursed and condemned, fills the soul with joy and peace.

Nevertheless, this peace of heart is by the sovereign will and pleasure of the Holy Spirit. A man may be chosen in the eternal love of the Father, redeemed by the blood of the Son and justified freely by the grace of God so that he has a right to all the promises of the gospel. Yet this person can, by no reasonings or persuasions of his own heart, by no considerations of the promises of the gospel, nor of the love of God or grace of Christ in them, be brought to that peace until it is produced in him by the Holy Spirit. 'Peace' is the fruit of the Spirit (*Gal. 5:22*).

THE HOLY SPIRIT BRINGS JOY TO THE HEARTS OF BELIEVERS

The Spirit is called 'the oil of gladness' (*Heb. 1:9*). His anointing brings gladness with it (*Isa. 61:3*). 'The kingdom of God is righteousness, peace and joy in the Holy Spirit' (*Rom. 14:17*). The Thessalonians received the word with joy in the Holy Spirit (*I Thess. 1:6; I Pet. 1:8*). To give joy to the hearts of believers is chiefly the work of the Holy Spirit. He enables believers to 'rejoice in hope of the glory of God' (*Rom. 5:2*). This joy is produced by the Spirit pouring into our hearts the love of God and so carrying them through every kind of tribulation (*Rom. 5:5*).

The Holy Spirit produces joy in the hearts of believers directly by himself without using any other means. As in sanctification he is a well of water springing up in the soul, so in 'comforting' he fills the souls and minds of men with spiritual joy. When he pours out the love of God in our hearts, he fills them with joy, just as he caused John to leap for joy in Elizabeth's womb when the mother of Jesus approached. This joy, the Holy Spirit works when and how he wills. He secretly injects this joy into the soul, driving away all fears and sorrows, filling it with gladness and causing it to exult, sometimes with unspeakable raptures of the mind.

The Holy Spirit produces joy in the hearts of believers by his other works with respect to us. He assures us of the love of God and of our acceptance with God and our adoption into his family. When we think about this, the Holy Spirit brings the truth home to us with joy. If we consider all the things the Holy Spirit does for us and in us, we will soon see what a strong foundation he lays in our hearts for our continual joy and gladness. Nevertheless, the Holy Spirit works joy in us as and when he pleases according to his sovereign will and pleasure. This way of producing joy in the heart, David describes as 'having his head anointed with oil' (*Psa. 23:5, 6*). And the result of this anointing, David says, is, 'surely goodness and mercy shall follow me all the days of my life'. In Isaiah we have a wonderful description of the work of the Comforter. (See Isaiah 35.)

THE HOLY SPIRIT BRINGS HOPE TO THE HEARTS OF BELIEVERS
(*Rom. 15:13*)

The great hope of the believer is to be like Christ and to enjoy God in Christ for ever. 'And,' says John, 'everyone who has this hope in him purifies himself, just as he is pure' (*I John 3:3*). By showing 'the things of Christ' to us and by 'glorifying Christ' in our hearts, the Holy Spirit arouses our desires to be like Christ and so we grow and increase in our hope, which is one way by which the Holy Spirit sanctifies us.

These are the general works of the Holy Spirit in the hearts of believers, which, if we consider them and all that they produce, will bring joy, assurance, boldness, confidence, expectation and glorying. We shall then see how much our whole communion with God is enriched and influenced by them.

21: *Satan's Attempts at Casting Contempt on the Holy Spirit*

The first way that Satan tried to cast contempt on the work of the Spirit was by setting up a ministry without the Spirit. This was done by setting up a liturgical service to be read by the minister. No special gift of the Spirit is required to do this. So men were set apart to the ministry who had never once 'tasted of the powers of the world to come' (*Heb. 6:5*), nor received any gifts of the Holy Spirit for the work of the ministry. Those who claimed to pray by the Spirit were held in contempt and scorn was poured upon them.

The second way that Satan tried to cast contempt on the work of the Spirit was by setting up the Spirit without a ministry. In the first case, it was sufficient for the Word to be read without either preaching or praying by the Spirit. Now the Spirit is enough without reading or studying the Word at all. In the first way, Satan allowed a literal embracing of what Christ had done in the flesh. Now he talks of Christ in the Spirit only, and denies that he ever came in the flesh. John warned Christians of this deceit (*I John 4:1*).

The first general work of the Spirit, as we have seen, is that he should bring back to our memories the things that Christ spoke for our guidance and comfort. This was to be the work of the Holy Spirit with respect to the apostles, who were to be the writers of Scripture. This is also his work with respect to believers to the end of the world. Now the things that Christ has spoken and done are 'written that we might believe, and believing, have life through his name' (*John 20:31*). They are written in Scripture. This, then, is the work of the Spirit which Christ has promised. He shall bring to our remembrance, and give us understanding of, the words of Christ in the Scripture for our guidance and comfort. Is this now the work of the Spirit which is abroad in the world and perverts many? The business of this false spirit is to deny the things that Christ has spoken which are written in the Word and, instead, to claim new revelations of his own, to lead men from the written Word in which the whole work of God and all the promises of Christ are recorded. Such was the spirit of the Montanists and that of Mohammed and of all who claim new revelations today.

The second general work of the Spirit is to glorify Christ (*John 16:14*). The Holy Spirit was to glorify him who was to suffer in Jerusalem. But the false spirit that is in the world glorifies itself. It denies and treats with contempt Christ who suffered for us. Its own glory and honour is all this false spirit seeks, wholly upsetting the order of the divine dispensations. The origins and source of all divine dispensations lay in the Father's love. The Son came to glorify the Father. He still says, 'I do not seek my own glory, but the glory of him that sent me'. The Son, having carried on the work of redemption, was now to be glorified with the Father. This is what he prayed for (*John 17:1*). So the Holy Spirit is sent, whose work it is to glorify the Son. But now a false spirit has come whose whole work is to glorify himself, not Christ. By this we can know what sort of spirit this is that is in the world.

The third general work of the Spirit is to pour into our hearts the love of God. By this, believers are filled with joy, peace and hope. What, then, is that spirit who brings men into bondage, who fills them with fear, creating in them anything but a childlike attitude to the Father? What is that spirit who makes himself a spirit of bondage and slavery in those in whom he is and a spirit of cruelty and persecution to others?

The fourth general work of the Spirit is to be a Spirit of prayer. What, then, is that spirit that teaches men to despise prayer as a base and contemptible way of communing with God?

In a word, it is an easy task to take all the great works of the Holy Spirit and to show that the false spirit of antichrist comes in direct opposition and contradiction to every one of them. In this way, Satan has passed from one extreme to another, from a bitter, wretched opposition to the Spirit of Christ to a cursed claim to be the true Spirit of God.

22: Preparation for Communion with the Holy Spirit

To encourage us to prepare ourselves for communion with the Holy Spirit, consider the works he came to do.

He brings comfort and strength to us in all our troubles and afflictions. Afflictions and troubles are what God has provided in his house for his children (*Heb. 12:5, 6*). And in all our afflictions, we need the comfort and strength of the Holy Spirit. Afflictions are not to be despised, because they are the chastisements of the Lord (*Heb. 12:5*).

Men often do despise afflictions. They think that the troubles that come on them are nothing. They refuse to see God's hand in them. They are well able to look after themselves in their troubles. So they do not seek the comfort and strengthening of the Holy Spirit.

Men often sink into despair under their trials and afflictions. So the Hebrew Christians are commanded to 'strengthen the hands which hang down, and the feeble knees' (*Heb. 12:12*). The first despise the help of the Holy Spirit through pride of heart, whereas the latter sink under the weight of their troubles. And which of these hands have we often let hang down?

Now there is no way of managing our souls in troubles and afflictions so that God is glorified and we ourselves spiritually strengthened but by the comforts of the Holy Spirit. All that Christ promised his disciples when he told them of the great troubles and persecutions they would have in the world is the Comforter. And this, Paul tells us, came to pass (*II Cor. 1:4–6*). So Paul says, 'We glory in tribulations' (*Rom. 5:3*). But how can we do this? By the Holy Spirit pouring out the love of God in our hearts (*Rom. 5:5*). So believers are said to receive the Word in affliction, with joy of the Holy Spirit (*I Thess. 1:6*). They are to 'take joyfully the spoiling of their goods'. All these we are enabled to do to the glory of God by the Comforter, the Holy Spirit.

THE HOLY SPIRIT BRINGS COMFORT TO US WHEN BURDENED WITH SIN

When the manslayer under the law had killed a man unawares and brought the guilt of blood upon himself, he fled to the city of refuge. Now our great and only refuge from the guilt of sin is the Lord Jesus Christ (*Heb. 6:17, 18*). In fleeing to him, the Holy Spirit brings great comfort to us.

A sense of sin fills the heart with troubles and sorrows. It is the Holy Spirit who gives us peace in Christ by pouring out the love of God into our hearts and by being a witness with our spirits that we are children of God. In this way, he removes all fears of God's wrath and answers the accusations of Satan and the law.

THE HOLY SPIRIT BRINGS STRENGTH AND COMFORT IN THE WHOLE COURSE OF OUR OBEDIENCE

The Holy Spirit enables believers to obey cheerfully, willingly and patiently to the end.

In a word, in all that concerns us in this life and in all our expectation of another life, we will always stand in need of the comfort and strength of the Holy Spirit.

Without the comfort and strength of the Holy Spirit, we will either despise afflictions or collapse under them and God's purpose in sending them to us will be defeated.

Without the comfort and strength of the Holy Spirit, sin will either harden us so that we treat it with contempt, or else cast us into despair and so we neglect the gracious means that God has graciously provided us with to defeat it.

Without the comfort and strength of the Holy Spirit, duties will either puff us up with pride or leave us without that joy which will encourage us to further obedience.

Without the comfort and strength of the Holy Spirit, prosperity will make us worldly and sensual in finding contentment in these things and so weaken us for the day of trial.

Without the comfort and strength of the Holy Spirit, the comforts of our loved ones will separate us from God and the loss of them will turn our hearts to stone.

Without the comfort and strength of the Holy Spirit, the poverty of the church will overwhelm us and the prosperity of the church will not concern us.

Without the comfort and strength of the Holy Spirit, we shall not have wisdom in our work, nor peace in any condition, nor strength for any duty, nor success in trial. Nor will we have joy and comfort in life, nor light in death.

How sad, then, is the condition of those who know nothing of the Spirit as Comforter.

HOW THE HOLY SPIRIT COMFORTS US

The Holy Spirit comforts us by communicating to us and acquainting us with the love of the Father. Christ assured the disciples of this. He said, 'The Father himself loves you' (*John 16:27*). He comforts us by persuading us of the eternal and unchangeable love of the Father. Such a soul may say, 'The world hates me, but my Father loves me. Men despise me as a hypocrite, but my Father loves me as a child. I am poor in this world, but I have a rich inheritance in the love of my Father. I mourn in secret under the power of my lusts and sins where no eyes see me, but the Father sees me and he is full of compassion. With this sense of his love, which is better than life, I rejoice in tribulation, glory in affliction and triumph as a conqueror. Though I am killed all day long, yet all my sorrows have a depth that can be fathomed and my trials have bounds which can be reached. But the breadth, depth and height of the love of the Father, who can measure that?'

The Holy Spirit comforts us by communicating to us and acquainting us with the grace of Christ. He brings to us the fruits he has purchased and shows us how desirable Christ is. The Holy Spirit glorifies Christ by revealing his excellences and his desirableness to believers. He reveals to believers that in Christ there is pardon of sin and deliverance from the curse and wrath to come. He shows them also that in Christ they are justified and adopted and are heirs to the numberless privileges accompanying the hope of glory given to them.

WHY THE HOLY SPIRIT COMFORTS US

The Holy Spirit comforts us because of his infinite love and willingness to help us in our utter weakness and helplessness. He knew what we were, what we would do and how we would deal with him. He knew we would grieve him and provoke him. He knew we would quench his activities in us and defile his dwelling place, and still he becomes our Comforter. Lack of a due consideration of this great love of the Holy Spirit weakens all the principles of our obedience. Did this knowledge abide in our hearts, how highly we would value his work as Comforter. As we value the love of Christ in laying down his life for our salvation, so we must value the work of the Holy Spirit as our Comforter. Yet how do we behave towards him? Are we not irritated, obstinate and unthankful? Do we not grieve, vex and provoke him? Yet in his love, he continues to do us good. Let us, then, by faith, meditate on this love of the Holy Spirit. He does this for us because he loves us and would have fellowship with us.

23: *The Behaviour of the Saints towards the Holy Spirit*

We are not to grieve him, nor quench him, nor resist him. We are not to grieve him, because he dwells in us. We are not to quench the things he wants to do in us. We are not to resist him in respect of the ordinances of Christ and his gifts for their ministration.

Do not grieve the Holy Spirit

The Holy Spirit cannot be grieved nor moved with sorrow. Grief implies change, weakness and disappointment. All these are incompatible with his infinite perfections. Yet men may actively do that which is able to grieve anyone who loves us, as does the Holy Spirit. If the Holy Spirit is not grieved, it is no thanks to us, but to his own unchangeable nature.

The Holy Spirit loves us and is concerned for our good. Therefore, when we sin, he is said to be grieved. So if we would not grieve him, we must consider the love, kindness and gentleness of the Holy Spirit to us.

We grieve the Holy Spirit by coming short of that complete sanctification which our being grafted into Christ requires. Therefore, if we would not grieve him, we must follow after holiness. Consider that the Holy Spirit, who is our Comforter is delighted with our obedience and grieved with our foolishness and the evils we do. Knowing this ought to stir us to a more perfect obedience.

Let this be our meditation: 'The Holy Spirit is infinite love and kindness to me. He has wonderfully chosen to be my Comforter. He does this work willingly, freely and powerfully. What great things I have received from him! How often he has comforted my soul! Can I live one day without him? Shall I not care what he wants to do in me? Shall I grieve him by my negligence, sin and foolishness? Shall not his love constrain me to walk before him in such a way that brings him great pleasure?' In this way, we shall have holy fellowship with him.

Do not quench the Spirit (I Thess. 5:19)

Some interpret this as suppressing spiritual gifts. They refer to verse 20: 'Do not despise prophesyings'. Others interpret this as 'the light that God has set up in our hearts'. But where is that light called absolutely 'the Spirit'?

It is the Holy Spirit that is meant, not his person, but his works. The Holy Spirit was typified by the fire that was always kept alive on the altar in the temple. He is also called a 'Spirit of burning'. Now when we want to resist fire, we quench it. So the opposition made to the Holy Spirit working in us is called 'quenching the Spirit,' as wet wood will do when it is cast into the fire. So we are said by the same picture to 'stir up with new fire' the gifts that are in us. The Holy Spirit is striving with us, working in us, encouraging growth in grace and the production of his holy fruit in us. 'Take heed,' says Paul, 'lest by the power of your lusts and temptations, you do not pay attention to him, but quench his works of good will in you.'

So we have communion with the Holy Spirit when we consider him, by faith, as the author of all that we need by grace, of all the good works in our hearts and of all the help we have in our wrestlings with sin. When we consider all this, we have holy fellowship with him.

Do not resist the Holy Spirit

Stephen tells the Jews that they 'resisted the Holy Spirit' (*Acts 7:51*). How did they resist the Holy Spirit? They resisted the Holy Spirit in the same way that their fathers did. And how did their fathers resist the Holy Spirit? They persecuted the prophets and slew them. Their opposition to the prophets in their preaching the gospel or their showing the way of the Just One was their resisting of the Holy Spirit. Now the Holy Spirit is said to be resisted when the preaching of the Word is held in contempt, because the gift of preaching the Word is from him. So when Christ promised the Spirit to his disciples to be present with them for the conviction of the world, he tells them he will give them a mouth and wisdom which their enemies would not be able to contradict or resist (*Luke 21:15*). So as seen in Stephen, they 'were not able to resist the wisdom and the Spirit by which he spoke' (*Acts 6:10*). So those who do not obey the Word preached in today's ministry, which the Holy Spirit has set up in the church, resist the Spirit.

When the Word of God is preached, the authority, wisdom and goodness of the Holy Spirit in setting up this ordinance is to be recognised and respected. For this reason, obedience is to be given to the Word when it is preached, because the Holy Spirit and he alone gives gifts for the Word to be preached. When this truth keeps us humble and dependent on the Holy Spirit, then we have holy fellowship with him in this ordinance.

24: *How to have Fellowship with the Holy Spirit*

When we worship, we worship the divine nature. So it is impossible to worship any one person in the Godhead and not worship the whole Trinity. The divine nature in all its infinite excellence, dignity and majesty and as the origin and cause of all things is common to all three persons in the Godhead.

When we pray to God the Father, we pray in the name of Jesus Christ. Yet the Son is prayed to and worshipped with the Father, even though he is especially mentioned at the end of the prayer as Mediator to the whole Trinity, or to God in three persons. When we pray to God the Father, we pray to all the three persons in the Godhead, because as the Father is God, so also the Son is God and the Holy Spirit is God.

Paul tells us that our worship is 'to the Father', that we come to the Father 'through Christ' and that we are helped to do this 'by the Spirit' (*Eph. 2:18*). Here each person in the Godhead is distinguished from the other two as to the works each has been appointed to do, but not as to their being the object of divine worship. The Son and the Holy Spirit are no less worshipped in our access to God than the Father himself. The grace of the Father, which we get by the mediation of the Son and the help of the Holy Spirit, is why we draw near to God. So when we worship and pray to one person of the Trinity, we worship and pray to all three.

These things being presupposed and understood, I say that we are to worship the Holy Spirit as a distinct person in the Godhead. Jesus said, 'You believe in God, believe also in me' (*John 14:1*). So as we believe in God, we also believe with the same divine faith in the Holy Spirit. And as we worship Christ, not because he is Mediator, but because he is God, so we worship the Holy Spirit, not because he is the Comforter, but because he is God. Yet his being the Comforter is a powerful motive to worship him as God. Only as we experience his gracious works as Comforter will we be stirred to worship him as our gracious and merciful God.

So as believers, let us learn to put our faith in the Holy Spirit as God the Comforter. Then we shall learn to respect him, worship him, serve him, wait for him, pray to him and praise him.

The Holy Spirit, revealing himself as the Comforter, ought to be especially honoured, and when he is not, he is especially sinned against. Ananias is said to lie to the Holy Spirit, not to God (*Acts 5:3*). Ananias should have honoured the Holy Spirit in that special gift of charity which he was outwardly professing. Not doing this, he sinned especially against him.

Let us, then, value highly all the comforting works of the Holy Spirit, seeing they are evidences to us of his love and power. Faith will take special notice of his kindness in all things. We grieve him when we take no notice of what he does. And of those of us who do recognise and show gratitude for what he does, how few there are that consider him as the Comforter and rejoice in him as they ought.

So when we experience any of his comforting work, faith ought to say, 'This is from the Holy Spirit. He is the Comforter, the God of all comfort and consolation. I know there is no joy nor peace, no hope nor comfort but that which he works and gives. And so that he might give me this comfort, he has willingly taken on himself the office of Comforter. He does it because he loves me, and that is why he continues to comfort me. I remember, also, that he is sent by the Father and Son to be the Comforter and consoler of distressed believers. It is from him that I have such joy. What price should I set on his love? How shall I value the mercy that I have received?'

Our fellowship or communion with the Holy Spirit should stir us to give him praise, thanks, glory, honour and blessing for the mercies and privileges we receive from him, as we do the Son for his work of redemption (*Rev. 1:5, 6*). Are not the same praises and blessing due to him who makes Christ's work of redemption effectual to us? The Holy Spirit undertook to be our Comforter with no less infinite love than the Son who took it on himself to be our Redeemer. When we feel our hearts warmed with joy, strengthened in peace and established in obedience, let us give him the praise that is due to him. Let us bless his name and rejoice in him.

The glorifying of the Holy Spirit by thanking him for his spiritual comforts is no small part of our communion with him. We also have communion with the Holy Spirit when we pray to him for his comfort. John prays for grace and peace from the seven Spirits that are before the throne, or the Holy Spirit, whose works are perfect and complete.

Consider the Holy Spirit as the one sent from the Father and the Son to be our Comforter. We should pray daily for the Holy Spirit from the Father in the name of Jesus Christ. This is the daily work of believers. They look upon, and by faith consider, the Holy Spirit as the one promised and as the one sent. In this promise, they know, lies all their grace, peace, mercy, joy and hope. For by him, as the one promised, and by him alone are these things communicated to believers. If, therefore, our living to the glory of God or the joy of such a life is important to us, then we are to ask for him from the Father as children ask their parents for their daily bread. It is in this asking and receiving of the Holy Spirit that we have communion with the Father, who in his love sent the Holy Spirit to us. We also have fellowship with the Son in his grace who purchased the Holy Spirit for us. And we also have fellowship with the Holy Spirit as the gift received from the Father and the Son.

Another way by which we have communion with the Holy Spirit is by humbling ourselves for our sins and disobedience. He have grieved him, quenched his works of grace and resisted him in his ordinances. Let our souls be humbled before him for these things.

Finally, what about unbelievers who know nothing of the Holy Spirit and his works of grace?

Unbelievers have no comfort or spiritual strength. They must bear their own burdens. And how are they able to do that if God presses his hand down on their burdens? Such people give an outward impression of being happy, whereas inwardly they are miserable.

All their determinations and resolutions are but attempts to resist God. They strive to be at peace under that which God has sent to disturb them. God does not afflict those who do not have the Spirit to exercise their patience, but to disturb their peace and security. All their arming themselves with patience and good resolutions is but to keep themselves in that false security from which God means to cast them out or else bring them nearer to eternal ruin. This is the best comfort in the time of their trouble.

If they have false assurance of God's care and promises to them, and in this false assurance they comfort themselves, then their comfort is like the dreams of a hungry man who thinks he is eating and drinking, but when he awakes, he is still hungry and thirsty. So, many will awaken in the last day and see all things clearly. In that day, they will then find that God is their enemy. They will see him laugh at their calamity. They will hear him mocking when their judgment comes on them to the full.

Unbelievers have no peace. They have no peace with God,

nor any peace in their own souls. The peace which the Holy Spirit gives is true and solid, so unbelievers who have not been made partakers of the Holy Spirit have no such peace. They may say, 'Peace, peace', but sudden destruction is at hand. Self-righteousness is what unbelievers trust in for peace, as may easily be proved, and this vain hope comes from their ignorance of God and a treacherous conscience. And what will this self-righteousness avail them in the day when the Lord deals with them?

The joy and hope of unbelievers are also false and perishing. Scripture tells us that unless the Spirit of Christ is in us, we are dead, we are reprobates, we are not Christ's people. Without him, we can experience none of those glorious works of his. If we profess to be believers, we must seriously examine ourselves to see whether we have truly received the Holy Spirit or not. If the Spirit does not dwell in you, if he is not your Comforter, then God is not your Father and nor is the Son your Redeemer. Nor do you have any part or lot in the riches of the gospel.

May God awaken some poor soul to consider this before the neglect and contempt of the Spirit gives rise to that despising of him from which there is no recovery. May the Lord show them the foolishness of their hearts, so that they may be ashamed and confounded and no longer act presumptuously.

THE WORKS OF JOHN OWEN

No outline can adequately summarise the significance of the life and work of John Owen (1616–1683). Summoned to preach before Parliament on several occasions, he was still only thirty-three when he addressed them on the day following the execution of King Charles I. A chaplain and adviser to Oliver Cromwell, he fell from the Protector's favour when he opposed the move to make him King. Even after the Great Ejection in 1662, he continued to enjoy some influence with Charles II who occasionally gave him money to distribute to impoverished ejected ministers. He was one of the leading Dissenters of his time.

It is, however, as an author that Owen is best known. During his lifetime he published over sixty titles of varying lengths; a dozen more appeared posthumously. Together they compose the twenty-four volume edition of his *Works* edited so ably by W. H. Goold in the mid-nineteenth century.

Owen's theology is marked by prodigious learning, profound thought and acute analysis of the human heart. Andrew Thomson, one of his biographers, says that Owen 'makes you feel when he has reached the end of his subject, that he has also exhausted it'. Both his subject matter – the great central themes of the Christian gospel – and his treatment of it – rich and satisfying, biblical and health-giving – secure him a permanent place in the galaxy of authors whose works deserve to be available for Christians in every age.

Owen's *Works* are published by the Banner of Truth Trust and are available as a set or in individual volumes. Contents of the twenty-three volumes are detailed overleaf.

CONTENTS OF THE TWENTY THREE
VOLUMES

DIVISION 1: DOCTRINAL

VOLUME 12

Vindiciae Evangelicae: or, the Mystery of the Gospel Vindicated
and Socinianism Examined.

Of the Death of Christ, and of Justification.

A Review of the Annotations of Grotius.

VOLUME 13

The Duty of Pastors and People Distinguished.

Eshcol: a Cluster of the Fruit of Canaan.

Of Schism; in Three Books.

Nonconformity Vindicated.

Tracts on the Power of the Magistrate, Indulgence, Toleration,
etc.

VOLUME 14

Animadversions on 'Fiat Lux'.

Vindications of Animadversions.

The Church of Rome no safe Guide.

On Union among Protestants.

The State and Fate of Protestantism.

VOLUME 15

Discourse concerning liturgies.

Discourse concerning Evangelical Love, Church Peace, and
Unity.

Inquiry concerning Evangelical Churches.

Answer to Dr. Stillingfleet on the unreasonableness of Separa-
tion.

Instruction in the Worship of God.

VOLUME 16*

True Nature of a Gospel Church.

Tracts on Excommunication, Church Censures, Baptism, etc.

On the Divine Original of the Scriptures.

Posthumous Sermons.

Indices.

*The Latin writings contained in the original volume 17 have not been
republished. Thus the volumes have been renumbered from 17 to 23

DIVISION 4: EXPOSITORY

VOLUME 17

Concerning the Epistle to the Hebrews.
Concerning the Messiah.
Concerning the Jewish Church.

VOLUME 18

The Sacerdotal Office of Christ.
A Day of Sacred Rest.
Summary of Observations on Hebrews.

VOLUME 19

Exposition of Hebrews, 1:1–3:6.

VOLUME 20

Exposition of Hebrews, 3:7–5:14.

VOLUME 21

Exposition of Hebrews, 6:1–7:28.

VOLUME 22

Exposition of Hebrews, 8:1–10:39.

VOLUME 23

Exposition of Hebrews, 11:1–13:25.

JOHN OWEN ON THE CHRISTIAN LIFE

Sinclair B. Ferguson

John Owen has long been recognised by evangelicals as one
of the greatest of all English-speaking theologians. Like
Augustine, whom he so admired, Owen's thinking touched
both the depths of sin and the heights of grace. Many of his
readers have come away from reading him on such themes as
temptation, or indwelling sin, feeling that Owen knew them
through and through.

Owen's teaching was always pastoral in its concern. His
writings address the fundamental issues Christians face in
every age: How can I live the Christian life? How am I to deal
with sin and temptation? How can I find assurance, and live for
the honour of Jesus Christ?

John Owen on the Christian Life expounds Owen's teaching
on these and related themes. Ministers, Christian leaders,
readers of Owen, and those who are daunted by the sheer
voluminousness of his writings will find this book an ideal
companion.

*Dr Sinclair B. Ferguson is a member of the Faculty of Westminster
Theological Seminary, Philadelphia, U.S.A.*

ISBN 0 85151 503 7
316pp., cloth-bound

For free illustrated catalogue please write to:
THE BANNER OF TRUTH TRUST
3 Murrayfield Road, Edinburgh EH12 6EL
P.O. Box 621, Carlisle, Pennsylvania, 17013, U.S.A.